Our Daily Bread

BIBLE

WORD SEARCH
& ACTIVITY BOOK

Our Daily Bread
Publishing™

Our Daily Bread Bible Word Search and Activity Book
© 2021 by Our Daily Bread Publishing

Requests for permission to quote from this book should be directed to: Permissions Department, Our Daily Bread Publishing, PO Box 3566, Grand Rapids, MI 49501, or contact us by email at permissionsdept@odb.org.

Scripture quotations, unless otherwise indicated, are from the Holy Bible, New International Version®, NIV®. Copyright © 1973, 1978, 1984, 2011 by Biblica Inc.™ Used by permission of Zondervan. All rights reserved worldwide. www.zondervan.com.

Cover and Interior design by Rob Williams, InsideOut Creative Arts, Inc.

ISBN: 978-1-64070-089-5

Printed in the United States of America
21 22 23 24 25 26 27 28 / 8 7 6 5 4

BASIC BIBLE FACTS

Provide the answers for these Bible basics.

1. The Bible contains this many books.

2. The number of books in the Old Testament.

3. The number of books in the New Testament.

4. This Bible book has the most chapters.

5. The "Hall of Faith" is found in this Bible book.

6. This book of the Bible contains the story of Noah's flood.

7. These four books of the Bible are the writings called the Gospels.

8. This man wrote the book of Acts.

9. This book was given to its writer when he was on an island.

10. These three books of the Bible contain the wisdom of Solomon.

———— *Answer key on page 110.* ————

WOMEN OF THE BIBLE WORD SEARCH

Words may be horizontal, vertical, or diagonal,
forward or backward, and may overlap.

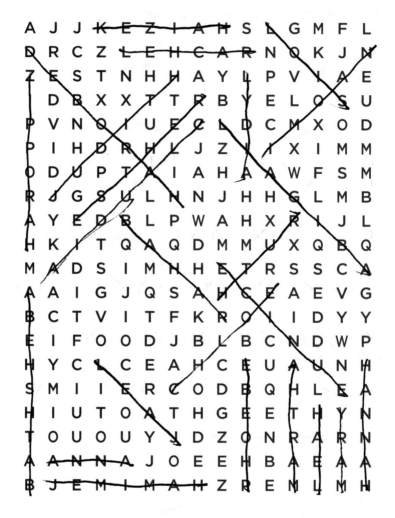

A J J K E Z I A H S L G M F L
D R C Z L E H C A R N O K J N
Z E S T N H H A Y L P V I A E
D B X X T R B Y E L O S U
P V N O I U E C L D C M X O D
P I H D R H L J Z I X I M M
O D U P T A I A H A A W F S M
R J G S U L N N J H H G L M B
A Y E B L P W A H X R I J L
H K I T Q A Q D M M U X Q B Q
M A D S I M H H E T R S S C A
A A I G J Q S A H C E A E V G
B C T V I T F K R O I D Y Y
E I F O O D J B L B C N D W P
H Y C L C E A H C E U A U N H
S M I I E R C O D B Q H L E A
H I U T O A T H G E E T H Y N
T O U O U Y D Z O N R A R N
A A N N A J O E E H B A E A
B J E M I M A H Z R E N L M H

ABIGAIL	ESTHER	KEZIAH	NAOMI
ANNA	EUNICE	LEAH	PHOEBE
BATHSHEBA	HANNAH	LOIS	RACHEL
CHLOE	JAEL	LYDIA	RAHAB
CLAUDIA	JEMIMAH	MARTHA	RUTH
DEBORAH	JUDITH	MARY	ZIPPORAH

MORE BASIC BIBLE FACTS

Provide the answers for these Bible basics.

1. As a group, this is the name for the first five books of the Bible.

2. This man is generally considered to be the author of those first five books.

3. This man is considered to be the primary writer of the book of Psalms.

4. The Old Testament was written in this language.

5. The New Testament was written primarily in this language.

6. This book of the Bible is the longest by word count.

7. This book of the Bible is the shortest by word count.

8. We are unsure who is the author of this New Testament book.

9. This important collection of Bible documents was found in caves in Israel in 1948.

10. True or False. The chapter numbers and verse numbers were found in the original Bible manuscripts.

Answer key on page 110.

THE EXODUS WORD SEARCH

Words may be horizontal, vertical, or diagonal,
forward or backward, and may overlap.

```
F S C M Z T D N A T S P M A L
M J T M T A R R E V O S S A P
I W H X T B P T N A N E V O C
R A D J E E N S A G U Q L K S
I Z C A D R I E B S E X U X T
A N H O Y N A I K U D Q T U E
M C H Z K A T R C F S A S A L
Z P L E I C R P L G A T R A B
E G Q A O L U A N R N K M H A
V Y N W K E C I O E A D W M T
K I C R N N R N M S A N C I Y
S X O N E E Q D E E L U N K Z
K X C D F D N U R S O I H A D
X L L F S A S B X R N M A H M
G O O E M V W E H Q B E P U D
G B S M T E C T A O N P C P Q
P O O B H L E O G W Z S G N O
M C E S M J R S A B B A T H I
```

AARON	JETHRO	RED SEA
ARK	LAMPSTAND	SABBATH
COMMANDMENTS	MANNA	SHEWBREAD
COVENANT	MOSES	SINAI
CURTAIN	OFFERINGS	TABERNACLE
EPHOD	PASSOVER	TABLETS
GOLDEN CALF	PRIEST	
INCENSE	QUAIL	

WHO SAID IT?

Identify the speaker of each Bible quotation.
One will be used more than once.

A. DAVID   D. JESUS   G. PAUL
B. ISAIAH   E. JOSEPH   H. RUTH
C. JAMES   F. MOSES AND AARON   I. SOLOMON

____ 1. "Your people will be my people and your God my God."

____ 2. "I can do all this through him who gives me strength."

____ 3. "Let my people go."

____ 4. "You meant evil against me; but God meant it for good."

____ 5. "The LORD is my shepherd, I shall not want."

____ 6. "Remember your Creator in the days of your youth, before the days of trouble come."

____ 7. "Love is patient, love is kind. It does not boast, it is not proud."

____ 8. "Those who hope in the LORD will renew their strength. They will soar on wings like eagles; they will run and not be weary."

____ 9. "The prayer of a righteous man is powerful and effective."

____ 10. "Come to me, all you who are weary and burdened, and I will give you rest."

—— Answer key on page 111. ——

KING DAVID CROSSWORD

What do you know about David,
ancestor of Jesus of Nazareth?

Across

1. Called a "man after God's own _____"

3. David's weapon of choice versus Goliath

7. David's best friend

9. Town where David was born

10. King before David

11. What Absalom got caught in a tree, killing him

12. David played this for King Saul, also called a lyre

14. Wife was angry when David did this before the Lord

16. Confronted David about his sin with Bathsheba

17. What David could not build but Solomon did

Down

2. David's son who tried to take the throne

4. Hometown of Goliath

5. Killed a lion and a bear while doing this job

6. David's father

7. City that David made Israel's capital

8. What David wanted to put in a temple instead
   of in a tent

13. The building David constructed in Jerusalem

15. Caves where David had a chance to harm Saul

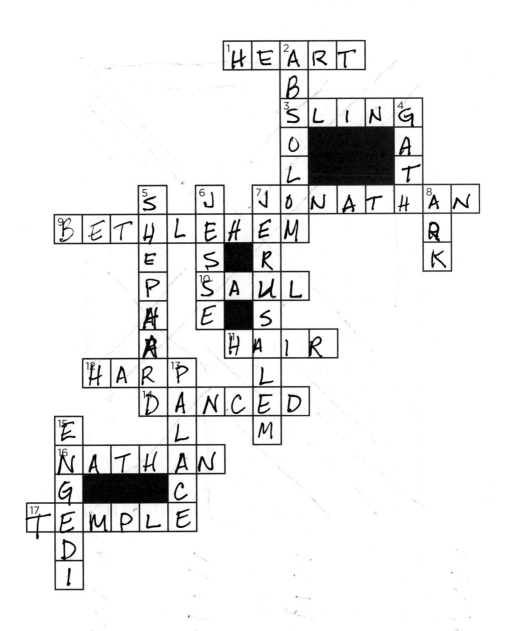

WONDERS OF NATURE IN
JOB 38 WORD SEARCH

Words may be horizontal, vertical, or diagonal,
forward or backward, and may overlap.

E S W M W G E X P A N S E S T
C U P I S Y M G R A I N W H C
V O S R E N L Y T Y D N U L L
H D N E I I O V Q V E N O I D
G A Q S A N Q W O F D U G A Z
Q R D H T C G C P E D H W A Q
R K X W M E I S R S T N R J G
V N E X G H L S W N G B A G B
D E Q T A C T L I X F Q X T W
P S W E V O T N A A T S A M I
B S X D R R G B E T R S O F N
A F I M E X R V R A L I O I D
S F S Z W Z Q N T S R O J R S
W B R X L D B S E O J Y N U F
D P Z X U U V D G T C N L S J
X Z E S M F A W T S R T Y O N
V Z T R F I Q H P E W E P A S
X G O O E G G A S V E R S M X
C T V L W I B K C A T C I E N
S D P D L T U B J W Y H I M D

CLOUDS DESERT LIGHT SPRINGS
CONSTELLATIONS ORION DUST STARS
THUNDERSTORMS EXPANSES PLEIADES STORM
LIGHTNING DARKNESS SNOW HAIL
FROST WAVES RAIN WINDS
DAWN ICE SEA

Answer key on page 112.

OLD TESTAMENT
CHRONOLOGY

Put the following sixteen Old Testament events
in chronological order (1–16).

____ A. Nehemiah reconstructs the wall of Jerusalem

____ B. The Israelites are taken to Babylon in exile

____ C. The fall of mankind

____ D. Ruth marries Boaz

____ E. David becomes Israel's second king

____ F. Joseph is sold into slavery

____ G. Noah enters the ark

____ H. Ezra returns from exile in Babylon

____ I. The people build the tower of Babel

____ J. Solomon builds the temple

____ K. Esther tells the king of Haman's plot

____ L. Moses and the burning bush

____ M. Joseph becomes second in command in Egypt

____ N. The Israelites are freed from Egypt

____ O. Daniel is thrown into the lion's den

____ P. Abraham leaves Ur of the Chaldees

ACTS 1—9 CROSSWORD

"All the believers were together and had everything in common. . . . And the Lord added to their number daily those who were being saved." —Acts 2:44, 47

Across

4. Wrote the book of Acts

5. Saul had Christians put here

6. For preaching the resurrection, Paul and John were this

9. Philip baptized a man from this country

10. The day the Holy Spirit came on the believers

12. The new Christians broke bread and did this

13. Jesus said believers would receive this through the Holy Spirit

14. Waiting on tables was the first job of these men in the church

15. Peter raised this woman from the dead

18. Visitors from other lands heard the disciples speak in their own this

19. As Stephen was martyred, this man approved

21. As a result of sin, Ananias and Sapphira did this

Down

1. At first, some Christians had this feeling about Paul

2. Through persecution, Christians from Jerusalem were this

3. The disciples chose him to replace Judas

7. Tongues of this fell on each person

8. After conversion, Paul (Saul) preached in these religious buildings

10. Preached the first evangelistic sermon

11. Disciples spoke in other this

14. Saul was going here when he saw a great light

16. This many thousand people were saved

17. This hid Jesus from the people's sight at His ascension

20. Ananias and Sapphira did this to God

BIBLE NUMBERS

Match the event with the number.

A. THREE   E. TWELVE   I. THREE HUNDRED
B. SEVEN   F. THIRTY-THREE   J. NINE HUNDRED
C. EIGHT   G. FORTY   SIXTY-NINE
D. NINE   H. ONE HUNDRED FIFTY

____ 1. Approximate earthly age of Jesus when He died.

____ 2. The number of people Jesus raised from the dead in the New Testament narrative.

____ 3. The Israelites marched around Jericho this many times on the seventh day before it fell.

____ 4. When Jesus fed the 5,000, the disciples picked up this many baskets full of leftovers.

____ 5. The Israelites wandered in the wilderness this many years before they crossed into the Promised Land.

____ 6. The number of days old a Jewish boy was to be when he was circumcised.

____ 7. When Gideon finally had to go to battle with the Midianites, he had this many soldiers.

____ 8. In Noah's time, the earth was covered with water once the rain stopped after the flood for this many days.

____ 9. Noah's grandfather Methuselah lived this many years before he died.

____ 10. When Jesus healed the ten lepers, this many men did not return to say thank you.

BIBLE FOODS WORD SEARCH

Words may be horizontal, vertical, or diagonal,
forward or backward, and may overlap.

APPLES
BARLEY
BEANS
BREAD
CORIANDER
CORN
CUCUMBERS
DATES
FIGS

FISH
GOAT
GRAPES
HONEY
LEEKS
MANNA
MILK
OLIVE OIL
OLIVES

ONIONS
PARTRIDGE
POMEGRANATES
QUAIL
RAISINS
SALT
STEW

— Answer key on page 114. —

BIRTH OF JESUS FILL-IN

Fill in the blank.

1. God sent the angel _____ to tell Mary that she was going to be Jesus's mother.

2. One of the things the angel told Mary was that her Son would be given the throne of "his father _____."

3. Mary protested upon hearing that she was going to have a baby, saying, "How can this be, since I am a _____?" (Luke 1:34)

4. After finding out that Mary was pregnant, Joseph was thinking about ending his relationship with her until an _____ appeared to him.

5. Joseph was told what to name the baby, and he was told that Jesus would _____ the people from their _____.

6. Late in Mary's pregnancy, she and Joseph had to travel from _____ to _____ because Joseph had to go to the town of his family to be registered.

7. After the shepherds saw Jesus lying in a manger, they went and told other people, who were _____ by what they heard.

8. When Mary and Joseph took Jesus to the temple for purification, there was man there who had been told he would not die until he saw the Messiah. When he did see Him, _____ took Him in his arms and praised God.

9. When Herod found out about the baby Jesus, he met with the _____ and told them to report back to him after they found Jesus.

10. An angel told Joseph that Herod was searching for Jesus, so he told the family of Jesus to escape to _____ to avoid the king.

Answer key on page 114.

MORE BIBLE NUMBERS

Match the event with the number.

A. FOUR
B. SEVEN
C. EIGHT
D. TEN

E. ELEVEN
F. TWELVE
G. THIRTEEN
H. THIRTY

I. NINETY-ONE
J. ONE THOUSAND

____1. In Revelation 4, John speaks of seeing this many "living creatures, and they were covered with eyes, in front and in back."

____2. In Matthew 25, Jesus told a parable about this many virgins who were waiting for the bridegroom.

____3. The number of pieces of silver Judas got for betraying Jesus.

____4. In the tabernacle in the wilderness, there were this many goat hair curtains used for the tent—each thirty cubits long and four cubits wide.

____5. The only number from 1 to 15 that does not appear in the New Testament.

____6. Sarah's approximate age when Isaac was born.

____7. In the book of Revelation, John wrote to this many specific churches.

____8. Before He was betrayed, Jesus had this many disciples.

____9. Using hyperbole, the psalmist said it is better to serve one day in the Lord's courts than this many days someplace else.

____10. Josiah was this many years old when he became king of Judah.

———— Answer key on page 114. ————

NAME THAT BOOK

Select the book of the Bible related to these questions.

1. The book of the Bible that tells the story of Paul's shipwreck.
   - a. Luke
   - b. Philippians
   - c. Acts
   - d. 2 Corinthians

2. The two books of the Old Testament that do not mention God.
   - a. Exodus
   - b. Ruth
   - c. Esther
   - d. Song of Songs

3. The book of the Bible that tells about the Israelites finally getting to cross the Jordan River and enter the Promised Land to live there.
   - a. Exodus
   - b. 1 Chronicles
   - c. 2 Chronicles
   - d. Joshua

4. The book of the Bible that tells about the rebuilding of the temple in Jerusalem.
   - a. Nehemiah
   - b. Ezra
   - c. Malachi
   - d. Jeremiah

5. This gospel is not like the others in stories and content, so it is not considered a "synoptic gospel."
   - a. Matthew
   - b. Mark
   - c. Luke
   - d. John

6. These books of the Bible were written by Jesus's brothers.
   a. Colossians
   b. Jude
   c. Acts
   d. James

7. This book of the Bible contains the following quote, "Meaningless, meaningless, . . . everything is meaningless."
   a. Song of Songs
   b. Ecclesiastes
   c. Proverbs
   d. Psalms

8. The book of the Bible that is noted for providing the people of that time a long list of laws and regulations plus instructions for worshiping God.
   a. Deuteronomy
   b. 2 Chronicles
   c. Leviticus
   d. Ecclesiastes

9. The book of the Bible that mentions the constellations the Bear, Pleiades, and Orion.
   a. Genesis
   b. Revelation
   c. Job
   d. Amos

10. The book of the Old Testament Jesus quotes from most often.
    a. Psalms
    b. Deuteronomy
    c. Isaiah
    d. Exodus

BOOKS OF THE OLD TESTAMENT WORD SEARCH

Words may be horizontal, vertical, or diagonal,
forward or backward, and may overlap.

```
H T C E L E I K E Z E G F J M
G P E H K N P Q Q L O Y O Z J
H E S X R A Y T W B H B G N D
E H N A O O S U C I T I V E L
F Z C E L D N X U W S R G A Q
P Q W N S M U I J M U G M A D
A R S P D I S S C T Q E N E P
E N E E V N S E H L N L U I G
S E G Z T G K E M T E T L W K
O H X S V S L D A M E S T F Y
H E M F A E A T A R E H T S E
X M A P I M I I O N T X B A A
B I L S A O U N S H I S M L R
N A A T N Q O E A E E E G I Z
S H C S Q M Z I L G L Z L U E
K O H J Y R A Z D Z J C D I X
G E I Z W S A U H S O J C F U
Q D G E I A J H A I M E R E J
```

CHRONICLES	HOSEA	MALACHI
DANIEL	ISAIAH	NEHEMIAH
DEUTERONOMY	JEREMIAH	PSALMS
ECCLESIASTES	JOB	RUTH
ESTHER	JOSHUA	SAMUEL
EXODUS	JUDGES	
EZEKIEL	KINGS	
EZRA	LAMENTATIONS	
GENESIS	LEVITICUS	

MORE WHO SAID IT?

Match the name with the person who said the following statements recorded in the Bible. One is used more than once.

A. DAVID
B. GIDEON
C. GOD
D. HANNAH

E. ISAIAH
F. JESUS
G. JOHN
H. MOSES

I. PAUL
J. SOLOMON

G 1. "If we confess or sins, he is faithful and just and will forgive us our sins."

F 2. "I am the way and the truth and the life."

E 3. "He was despised and rejected by mankind, a man of suffering, and familiar with pain."

H 4. "God created man in his own image, in the image of God he created him."

I 5. "For I am not ashamed of the gospel."

C 6. "Where were you when I laid the foundation of the earth?"

A 7. "Have mercy on me, O God, . . . Against you, you only, have I sinned."

B 8. "I will place a wool fleece on the threshing floor. If there is dew only on the fleece and all the ground is dry, then I will know that you will save Israel by my hand."

J 9. "Fear God and keep his commandments; for this is the duty of all mankind."

D 10. "I am a woman who is deeply troubled. I have not been drinking wine or beer; I was pouring my soul out to the Lord."

Answer key on page 115.

THE KINGS OF THE UNITED MONARCHY
& JUDAH WORD SEARCH

Words may be horizontal, vertical, or diagonal,
forward or backward, and may overlap.

```
L S H N S H A I Z A H A Q L A
Q J O S I A H O A W Q J J G S
F N I H C A I O H E J E I A W
A J B Z V A H A Z Z H H U A S
V X O R U I O V Y O A L R O X
B Q P A F B M V S I W E L G W
A Q S A S C E H Z V H O X J J
H S W B P H A Z X O M L H T G
A L A I B P U M B O N O M A H
I K N J H E M O N W A Y S M N
K H A A G M A I J A H E A Z A
E A T H M M K E K A H N C A N
Z I F S Q A H E I A A V A H Q
E K O V M O H L P S I B H A Q
H E Z P R H A T S I Z O E O J
F D D A K H G E O J A B H H O
M E M X T P H Z H J M S Y E N
T Z L A L H X B A E A N Q J J
```

ABIJAH	ATHALIAH	JEHOSHAPHAT	SAUL
AHAZ	HEZEKIAH	JOASH	SOLOMON
AHAZIAH	JEHOAHAZ	JOSIAH	UZZIAH
AMAZIAH	JEHOIACHIN	JOTHAM	ZEDEKIAH
AMON	JEHOIAKIM	MANASSEH	
ASA	JEHORAM	REHOBOAM	

WHERE IS THAT STORY IN THE BIBLE?

In what book of the Bible would you look to find
the following stories?

1. Saul becoming Israel's first king

2. Peter getting out of prison while his friends were praying
   for him

3. Jesus teaching in the temple at age twelve

4. Abraham leaving his homeland at God's request

5. The giving of the Ten Commandments

6. Elijah being taken to heaven in a "chariot of fire"

7. King Belshazzar's banquet where the people saw the
   handwriting on the wall

8. Jesus turning water into wine at a wedding in Cana

9. Achan taking what didn't belong to him at Jericho, lead-
   ing to a stunning defeat for Israel at Ai

10. Deborah and her leadership in the battle against Sisera

——— Answer key on page 116. ———

PEOPLE IN JESUS'S LIFE

Match the people who appeared in Jesus life
with their description.

A. ANNA   E. JOHN THE   H. SIMEON
B. ELIZABETH   BAPTIST   I. SIMON PETER
C. JAIRUS   F. MARTHA   J. ZACCHAEUS
D. LEGION   G. MATTHEW

_____ 1. Mary's relative, who was pregnant at the same
      time as Mary.

_____ 2. The man who held baby Jesus in his arms and
      praised God for His arrival.

_____ 3. An eighty-four-year-old woman who saw baby Jesus
      in the temple and told a lot of people about Him.

_____ 4. The first disciple Jesus called on to follow Him,
      according to Matthew 4:18–19.

_____ 5. The tax collector at whose house Jesus ate, causing
      the Pharisees to criticize Jesus.

_____ 6. The good friend (and relative) of Jesus who was
      beheaded by Herod the tetrarch.

_____ 7. The name of the demon-possessed man Jesus
      healed in the region of the Gerasenes.

_____ 8. The synagogue ruler whose twelve-year-old daugh-
      ter Jesus raised from the dead.

_____ 9. The sister from Bethany who was busy with house-
      work while her sister sat Jesus's feet.

_____ 10. A tax collector who climbed a tree to see Jesus pass
      through town—and Jesus spotted him in that tree.

24

QUOTING PAUL

Finish each of these verses with one word.

1. "The righteous will live by _____."
   Romans 1:17

2. "The message of the cross is _____ to
   those who are perishing." 1 Corinthians 1:18

3. "For I am not ashamed of the _____."
   Romans 1:16

4. "I resolved to know nothing while I was with you except
   Jesus Christ and him _____."
   1 Corinthians 2:2

5. "Don't you know that you yourselves are God's temple
   and that God's _____ lives in you?"
   1 Corinthians 3:16

6. "We are _____ for Christ." 1 Corinthians 4:10

7. "Do you not know that your _____ are
   temples of the Holy Spirit?" 1 Corinthians 6:19

8. "Love is _____, love is kind." 1 Corinthians 13:4

9. "When I became a man, I put the ways of _____
   behind me." 1 Corinthians 13:11

10. "If Christ had not been raised, your faith is
    _____." 1 Corinthians 15:17

Answer key on page 116.

BOOK OF REVELATION CROSSWORD

"Blessed is the one who reads aloud the words of this prophecy, and blessed are those who hear it and take to heart what is written in it, because the time is near."
—Revelation 1:3

Across

4. The name of a great ancient city is used in chapters 17 and 18. Revelation 18:2 says, "Fallen! Fallen is _____ the great"

6. In Revelation 20:11, John saw a great white _____

7. Where the writer was when he penned Revelation

10. New heaven and new _____

11. John saw *this* coming from the sea. It had ten horns and seven heads (Revelation 13:1)

12. The church at Ephesus had lost their first _____

Down

1. The first word said by the four living creatures in Revelation 4:8

2. Revelation 22:21 says, "The _____ of the Lord Jesus be with God's people. Amen"

3. The human writer of the book of Revelation

5. In chapter eight seven angels had seven _____

8. What the message to the seven churches was written on

9. In chapters 6 and 7, the Lamb opened seven _____

THE KINGS OF THE UNITED MONARCHY & ISRAEL WORD SEARCH

Words may be horizontal, vertical, or diagonal,
forward or backward, and may overlap.

```
M  U  B  J  E  N  V  Z  A  H  A  O  H  E  J
A  E  C  H  V  L  C  H  A  I  H  A  K  E  P
S  Z  N  Q  S  D  A  M  A  O  B  O  R  E  J
F  A  I  A  P  K  N  H  Z  N  A  D  A  B  J
K  B  B  M  H  D  C  I  L  X  S  Q  S  E  H
L  A  A  Q  R  E  M  S  W  T  V  B  H  O  B
X  W  D  H  N  I  M  W  R  J  A  O  S  N  C
Y  N  A  R  A  S  M  F  H  A  A  H  K  J  Z
I  J  V  G  X  R  O  O  S  S  E  H  C  O  O
H  G  I  P  O  S  U  H  H  A  H  S  M  E  F
A  M  D  I  I  T  A  G  R  A  I  R  H  S  K
I  A  C  E  C  P  N  L  K  C  I  Q  N  X  O
R  R  B  E  Q  R  O  E  U  I  U  Z  S  J  Q
A  O  H  H  J  E  P  N  Z  A  B  S  A  T  X
H  J  Q  S  H  A  L  L  U  M  S  U  U  H  H
C  Q  O  Q  V  N  L  Y  O  X  H  Z  H  W  A
E  R  J  H  D  Q  S  I  J  Q  R  F  Y  E  G
Z  K  K  P  F  H  S  O  L  O  M  O  N  S  J
```

AHAB	JEHOAHAZ	NADAB	SOLOMON
AHAZIAH	JEHOASH	OMRI	ZECHARIAH
BAASHA	JEHU	PEKAH	ZIMRI
DAVID	JEROBOAM	PEKAHIAH	
ELAH	JORAM	SAUL	
HOSHEA	MENAHEM	SHALLUM	

NAME THAT BIBLICAL LOCATION

Name the location that goes with each of the
following descriptions.

1. Where Jesus spoke in the synagogue and where he
   healed Peter's mother-in-law.

2. The hometown of Mary, Martha, and Lazarus.

3. The location where Elijah called down fire while in
   battle with Baal.

4. The name of the place where Jesus and His disciples
   prayed on the night He was betrayed.

5. Jesus was in the region of this two-word city when
   he asked the disciples, "Who do people say the Son
   of Man is?"

6. Where Moses went to receive the Ten Commandments
   from God.

7. Where the people of Judah were taken into captivity
   seventy years beginning in 586 BC.

8. (a) Where God wanted Jonah to go to preach to the
   people, and (b) where he went first instead.

9. The town Naomi and Ruth went to after their tragic
   losses in Moab.

10. Where the Holy Spirit led Jesus and where the devil
    found Him and tempted Him.

ANIMALS AND OTHER BIBLE CRITTERS
WORD SEARCH

Words may be horizontal, vertical, or diagonal,
forward or backward, and may overlap.

```
U S N P G A T I G V C G Z J I
E V N D Z E S H N A Z D X V
W L G G O C T I A P M F U V W
D I E W F D O H T T E G O R F
P P L V L Z R I E V L K L X Z
L D K B I C K H P R E F D H W
O I Z J J A Y T D D O E S K S
C H O S H S T Q U S L N Z N G
M O O N J W D H N G B E A H G
Y V W X H P J D A S G K O O M
Z S S Y L Y Q E O N E I A H Z
C D H I F C P D Y R Q T I C R
Y R V X X X Y Q H B A W U Q S
E A D V U L T U R E O V C H Y
R P C S W E A S E L E B E G D
P O S P A R R O W V M E P N E
S E E U H S I F O V P J I Y J
O L W M O Z I D N C P R A E B
```

BEAR	FROG	OSPREY	SPARROW
CAMEL	GNAT	OWL	STORK
COW	GOAT	OX	VULTURE
DOVE	HERON	PIG	WEASEL
EAGLE	LEOPARD	RAVEN	
FISH	LEVIATHAN	SHEEP	
FOX	LION	SNAKE	

KNOW YOUR BIBLE SECTIONS

One way to divide the Bible into sections is to categorize them by type of writing:

A. LAW   D. MAJOR PROPHETS   G. ACTS
B. HISTORY   E. MINOR PROPHETS   H. EPISTLES
C. WISDOM   F. GOSPELS   I. REVELATION

See if you can match the section to the details given below.

____ 1. The story of Hosea and Gomer

____ 2. John's vision of the future from the island of Patmos

____ 3. Solomon's great sayings

____ 4. The story of the exodus of God's people from Egypt

____ 5. The calling of the disciples

____ 6. The songs and poems of David and others

____ 7. The story of the Babylonian captivity and return to Israel

____ 8. The most complete story of the beginnings of the Christian church

____ 9. The Beatitudes of Jesus

____ 10. The great prophecy of Jesus's birth in Bethlehem

____ 11. The story of the creation of the world

____ 12. Jonah's adventures in Nineveh

____ 13. The details of Saul's persecution and then his salvation

____ 14. The promise of a new heaven and new earth

____ 15. The story of Abraham moving from Ur to the area of the Promised Land

____ 16. The details about church leadership in the Christian church

____ 17. Daniel's stories of heroism

____ 18. Nehemiah's concern for rebuilding the wall of Jerusalem

____ 19. The story of Jesus's birth, life, death, and resurrection

____ 20. The rise of the kingdom era of Israel and Judah

Answer key on page 118.

THE DISCIPLES OF JESUS

Fill in the blank.

1. The first two disciples Jesus chose to follow Him

2. Peter and Andrew were brothers. Name the other brother duo who were disciples

3. The nickname Jesus had for James and John

4. The disciple who was a tax collector

5. The disciple also called Didymus, which means "the twin"

6. The disciple charged with keeping track of their money

7. After Jesus's ascension to heaven, the disciples voted to replace Judas with this man

8. "The disciple whom Jesus loved" (John 13:23)

9. In a list of the disciples, these names would appear twice

10. This disciple wrote five books of the Bible

Answer key on page 119.

HOLY WEEK WORD SEARCH

Words may be horizontal, vertical, or diagonal,
forward or backward, and may overlap.

```
X N E N A M E S H T E G D P U
I A H D I I X R O O S T E R N
R X U O O S N P C H Z T I E F
P E F T S N U H F E E V E X V
P R S U H A K S A R L B G R L
P H A U K O N E E R S P E I R
L P A Y R L R N Y J R V M F F
I H L R E R U I A N O E G E B
S U I F I R E V T S S E S R T
I P N S D S Z C S Y L A A T L
G I R E P S E A T B N N D J F
N L B E Y D P E A I C B H U G
S A D C G B H R S H O E V S J
N T E U R U A W E D L N W W A
R E I D H P I S R I N O M I S
O X R D A N O I N T E D N O R
H T U A Q A L D Y N A H T E B
T Z B S A F G L A Y A R T E B
```

ANOINTED	GETHSEMANE	PRAYER
ARREST	HOSANNA	RESURRECTION
AUTHORITY	JESUS	ROOSTER
BETHANY	JUDAS	SADDUCEES
BETRAYAL	PARABLE	SIGN
BRANCHES	PASSOVER	SIMON
BURIED	PETER	TEMPLE
DONKEY	PHARISEES	THORNS
FIG	PILATE	

THE BEATITUDES FILL-IN

Fill in the blanks in the following quotes from the
Beatitudes (Matthew 5:3–10).

1. Blessed are the poor in _____,
   for theirs is the kingdom of heaven

   Blessed are those who mourn,
2. for they will be _____.

3. Blessed are the _____,
   4. for they will inherit the _____.

5. Blessed are those who _____ and thirst for
   righteousness,
   for they will be filled

Blessed are the merciful,
   6. for they will be shown _____.

7. Blessed are the _____ in heart,
   8. for they will see _____.

9. Blessed are the _____,
   for they will be called children of God.

10. Blessed are those who are _____ because
    of righteousness,
    for theirs is the kingdom of heaven.

HEAVEN WORD SEARCH

Words may be horizontal, vertical, or diagonal,
forward or backward, and may overlap.

```
Y K G V M U E Y L S L E G N A
G B Z O J Z A Q A S R E D L E
B Q W H L Z Y J M U R X D F H
S S Z S J D Q E B A X E A J T
A A A X O B T S C K G U V E K
Q G P F T T U S Q B V M I W
E R A P P E F S D D T P G R R
P E E T H Z S J C L L K R G I
M M Y D E I E A A E A F V X D
W X A O E I R T R S F R G I O
O T R E E E P E N K P K E L G
X T U G Y M M J Y R Q E P M P
O P L H N E S E T A G M R E E
Z V B L N I O W D O Z A A G Z
X Z N O O W G G P R B R W S H
W L R L N R M N I F L M P N N
E H Y X W R C F I S T H G I L
T M I L R D D S G S U P S J C
```

AGATE	GOLD	RIVER
ANGELS	JASPER	SAPPHIRE
ARK	JESUS	SCROLL
ELDERS	LAMB	SINGING
EMERALD	LIGHT	TEMPLE
GATES	PEARLS	THRONE
GOD	REDEEMED	TREE

BIBLE FIRSTS

Use the list to find the person who was responsible for the "Bible first" that is associated with him.

A. SOLOMON
B. ENOCH
C. ISAAC
D. MELCHIZEDEK

E. NIMROD
F. NOAH
G. OTHNIEL
H. REHOBOAM

I. SAUL
J. STEPHEN

____ 1. First martyr

____ 2. Built the first altar

____ 3. First judge of Israel

____ 4. First priest mentioned in the Bible

____ 5. Built the first temple in Jerusalem

____ 6. Name of the first city mentioned in the Bible

____ 7. First king of the Southern Kingdom of Judah

____ 8. First hunter mentioned in the Bible

____ 9. First person who was tied up

____ 10. First king of Israel

Answer key on page 120.

BIBLE "MOUNTS" OF SIGNIFICANCE

Match the Bible mount with the significant event
that happened there.

A. MOUNT ARARAT
B. MOUNT CARMEL
C. MOUNT GILBOA
D. MOUNT MORIAH
E. MOUNT NEBO
F. MOUNT OF BEATITUDES

G. MOUNT OF OLIVES
H. MOUNT OF
   TRANSFIGURATION
I. MOUNT SINAI
J. MOUNT ZION

____ 1. Abraham nearly sacrificed Isaac

____ 2. Moses saw the Promised Land

____ 3. Jesus gave the Sermon on the Mount

____ 4. Eastern hill of Jerusalem; taken from Jebusites
   by David

____ 5. Elijah defeated Baal

____ 6. Noah and family landed

____ 7. Moses received the Ten Commandments

____ 8. Elijah and Moses met with Jesus

____ 9. Saul and Jonathan died

____ 10. Jesus ascended to heaven

——— Answer key on page 120. ———

WOMEN OF THE BIBLE CROSSWORD

"A woman who fears the LORD is to be praised."
—Psalm 31:30

Across

3. Went out to draw water, discovered by Abraham's servant.

7. Bad girl of OT before redemption; made it into Jesus's genealogy.

9. Laughed when she heard she was going to have a baby in her old age.

10. Saved a race of people by confronting her husband the king.

12. She fell in love with Samson but eventually betrayed him.

13. Lost two sons to death; her daughter-in-law found a husband in Bethlehem.

15. Working in the fields when her future husband noticed her.

17. Thought Jesus was a gardener—until He said her name.

18. Saved her husband Nabal's life by preparing food for David and his men.

19. Unkind to Hannah when she couldn't get pregnant.

20. Sold items of purple; among first Christians in Thyatira.

Down

1. Refused to parade before her husband the king and his friends.

2. While in her garden, she ate some fruit she wasn't supposed to eat.

4. The mother of John the Baptist.

5. Opened the door and saw Peter—and was surprised.

6. Daughter of Laban, wife of Jacob.

8. Known for being a good seamstress who looked out for the needy.

11. Lied about a gift to the church; this cost her life.

14. Daughter of Saul; wife of Israel's second king.

16. She and husband were good friends of Paul.

17. Sang a song of praise after Red Sea crossing.

HOW'S THAT SPELLED?

Select the proper spelling for each of the
following Bible names.

____ 1. a. Melkizedech
         b. Melchisadek
         c. Melchizedek

____ 2. a. Nebuchunezzer
         b. Nebuchadnezzar
         c. Nebuchednezer

____ 3. a. Zerubbabel
         b. Zerubabble
         c. Zereububel

____ 4. a. Mephibosheth
         b. Mephibashath
         c. Mephebesheth

____ 5. a. Zechariah
         b. Zecheriah
         c. Zechireah

____ 6. a. Morducai
         b. Mordecai
         c. Mordakiah

____ 7. a. Delillah
         b. Dallilah
         c. Delilah

____ 8. a. Zacheas
         b. Zacchaeus
         c. Zacheus

____ 9. a. Absalam
         b. Absulum
         c. Absalom

____ 10. a. Ebenezer
         b. Ebennezar
         c. Ebeeneezer

——— Answer key on page 121. ———

BOOKS OF THE NEW TESTAMENT
WORD SEARCH

Words may be horizontal, vertical, or diagonal, forward or backward, and may overlap.

```
W  N  O  I  T  A  L  E  V  E  R  D  X  H  U
D  S  J  B  I  H  S  W  E  R  B  E  H  D  P
L  S  N  A  I  S  S  O  L  O  C  S  V  S  T
A  C  T  S  A  O  F  W  Q  W  E  Y  U  H  K
Y  N  C  F  P  H  I  L  E  M  O  N  E  P  T
P  H  I  L  I  P  P  I  A  N  S  S  G  I  I
X  V  X  P  H  I  Q  J  E  U  S  T  T  C  P
R  U  P  E  P  L  S  V  T  A  R  U  S  B  W
Q  X  R  T  E  J  A  I  L  O  S  N  F  O  G
Y  U  H  E  H  O  M  O  M  S  A  G  Y  A  J
X  U  N  R  O  O  N  A  N  I  D  W  L  U  Z
W  R  P  V  T  I  N  A  H  T  T  A  D  J  A
E  G  T  H  A  S  I  T  G  B  T  E  R  O  X
H  J  Y  N  I  S  N  G  Z  I  Z  N  B  N  A
T  T  S  K  E  I  B  W  A  Z  M  E  H  I  R
T  I  K  H  R  K  N  N  V  U  T  K  P  O  K
A  T  P  O  Q  A  S  V  C  B  V  U  Q  H  J
M  E  C  V  C  T  M  P  J  G  P  L  V  P  K
```

ACTS	JOHN	PHILIPPIANS
COLOSSIANS	JUDE	REVELATION
CORINTHIANS	LUKE	ROMANS
EPHESIANS	MARK	THESSALONIANS
GALATIANS	MATTHEW	TIMOTHY
HEBREWS	PETER	TITUS
JAMES	PHILEMON	

Answer key on page 122.

MORE ANIMALS AND OTHER BIBLE CRITTERS WORD SEARCH

Words may be horizontal, vertical, or diagonal, forward or backward, and may overlap.

```
M K U Y E F G R L R R M W M G
P A R T R I D G E S A V F R F
Y A G A Z E L L E D M D A B J
T Q D A R B O C A A O S C W C
I K W A H O Y V G S S E G O G
B D W E X K L V T H J I V R I
B F W D Q Z P R O X J J K M W
A Q G B V N I P S D R A Z I L
R C B W G C P V O C Q Q L W V
D N D A H E A T H P Y E G Y H
J O P I R N Z L H X Q G E P A
O E G U T A I N V G G C G P E
T L J Y M E B R J L P U J B D
S E P E S Z K X C O A H Z M P
W M O K I R Z C G L B K Z A N
E A P N A I V L I J L W C L G
W H W O L L A W S R Z U H A B
E C B D O G I H K W C O B O J
```

ANT	CRICKET	HAWK	RABBIT
APE	DOG	JACKAL	RAM
BOAR	DONKEY	LAMB	SWALLOW
BULL	EWE	LIZARD	WORM
CHAMELEON	GAZELLE	OSTRICH	
COBRA	GRASSHOPPER	PARTRIDGE	

PUTTING THE TEN COMMANDMENTS IN ORDER

Can you put these commandments in the order given to us in Scripture?

____ A. You should not misuse the name of the Lord.

____ B. Honor your father and mother.

____ C. You should not commit murder.

____ D. You should have no other gods before the one true God.

____ E. You should not steal.

____ F. You should not commit adultery.

____ G. You should not make any idols to worship.

____ H. Remember the Sabbath day.

____ I. You should not covet your neighbor's stuff.

____ J. You should not lie.

Answer key on page 123.

JACOB'S FAMILY WORD SEARCH

Words may be horizontal, vertical, or diagonal,
forward or backward, and may overlap.

```
J O J E B R A H C A S S I O D
D X J Z K X Z N X T R G C J A
R Z S O G Q N H I F U I R S Q
E E P D S W C I Q S K U H Z J
B D U H S E D H M B A E B A S
E I Y B J T P V L S R N C N G
K N N P M V Q H E Q U O A Q B
A A F B C X K H F U B P Z G T
H H M Q B S Y D A J H X M W O
N S M F I S A A C T U A F H B
Q Z E B U L U N A H K V H A I
D T X O H E J L I B A T S E L
B Y O I N L I S N M F P O L H
L C B K E E D M U O A C L S A
I G B K B H D A U O E J L I A
U O H O U C K E G R W M N D Z
O Z N Z E A K Q O A C N I E U
I P J Y R R V C J Y F D G S B
```

ASHER   ISAAC   RACHEL
BENJAMIN   ISSACHAR   REBEKAH
BILHAH   JACOB   REUBEN
DINAH   JOSEPH   SIMEON
ESAU   LEAH   ZEBULUN
GAD   NAPHTALI   ZILPAH

HOW ARE THEY RELATED?
OLD TESTAMENT

For each of the following pairs of people,
tell how the first person is related to the second person
(example: Abel - Adam, son - father).

1. Methuselah   Noah

_____   _____

2. Shem   Noah

_____   _____

3. Terah   Isaac

_____   _____

4. Rachel   Esau

_____   _____

5. Boaz   Naomi

_____   _____

6. Obed   Ruth

_____   _____

7. Obed   David

_____   _____

8. Aaron   Moses

_____   _____

9. Elkanah   Samuel

_____   _____

10. Rehoboam   Solomon

_____   _____

Answer key on page 123.

HOW ARE THEY RELATED?
NEW TESTAMENT

For each of the following pairs of people,
tell how the first person is related to the second person
(example: Abel - Adam, son - father).

1. James   Jesus

_____   _____

2. Peter   Andrew

_____   _____

3. Zechariah   John the Baptist

_____   _____

4. Aquila   Priscilla

_____   _____

5. Lazarus   Martha

_____   _____

6. Elizabeth   John the Baptist

_____   _____

7. Salome   Apostle John

_____   _____

8. James   Zebedee

_____   _____

PLACES JESUS VISITED WORD SEARCH

Words may be horizontal, vertical, or diagonal,
forward or backward, and may overlap. Ignore spaces.

```
P Y W O H C I R E J D M Z Z T
N S S D L E I F N I A R G G V
X B D F F N M E H E L H T E B
T E M P L E I J B E P N C T J
N X M S L C J N G E R Y T H X
C J D B S L H Y O O B Y O S V
I A E I E P P O E D I A A E L
R J P R M T T W R N I A N M H
E G W E U M H A N A V S A A T
V A F N R S N S Q L Z U I N E
I D Y C E N A R A A X I J E R
R A L B C A A L Y I O F N S A
N R H I M M P U E C D A K O Z
A E W N W X P M M M R A N A A
D N I S E U G O G A N Y S A N
R E K G W I L D E R N E S S C
O S Y E D I S N I A T N U O M
J C E E L I L A G G S B X R O
```

JORDAN RIVER	WILDERNESS	JERUSALEM
MOUNTAINSIDE	NAZARETH	EGYPT
NAIN	SYNAGOGUES	CHORAZIN
JERICHO	SIDON	TYRE
CAPERNAUM	GALILEE	GETHSEMANE
BETHSAIDA	GRAINFIELDS	CANA
TEMPLE	BETHLEHEM	GADARENES

HOW WELL DO YOU KNOW PSALM 23?

Fill in the blanks in Psalm 23.

1. The Lord is my _____, I lack _____.

2. He makes me lie down in _____ _____, he leads me beside _____ _____, he refreshes my _____.

3. He guides me along the right _____ for his name's sake.

4. Even though I _____ through the _____ valley, I will fear no _____, for you are with me; your _____ and your _____ they comfort me.

5. You prepare a _____ before me in the presence of my _____. You _____ my head with _____; my _____ overflows.

6. Surely _____ and _____ will follow me all the _____ of my life, and I will dwell in the _____ of the _____ forever.

—— Answer key on page 124. ——

THEOLOGY TERMS WORD SEARCH

Words may be horizontal, vertical, or diagonal,
forward or backward, and may overlap.

```
O M N I P O T E N T S H S O S
C J T N E P E R O G A C I O A
T O D Z X G T P I C O J V H S
X V V F R E N F R Y L E D Y H
I T M E S I T I J A R L C E S
E N E Y N S H I L E Y E A A Q
L O R Q J A N E I L H E L F R
W I C O T G N G L P E V R C U
N S Y T V N N T O L A W R Y H
O S H I X T E R M T G E D E U
I E O T Y F P S I S C X A N W
T C L H E I A O E N I V H P I
A R I E X E N I A R E T G M D
L E N L A H E R T N P J P D D
E T E V M C U T Y H A I F A K
V N S R A S K I M C V V N R B
E I S R S O R A P T U R E M H
R C G A B L N X E S I G X V O
```

ASSURANCE
BAPTISM
COVENANT
FAITH
FALL
GIFTS
GRACE
HEAVEN

HELL
HOLINESS
INDWELLING
INTERCESSION
MERCY
OMNIPOTENT
OMNIPRESENT
PRAYER

PROPHECY
RAPTURE
REPENT
REVELATION
SALVATION
SOVEREIGNTY
TITHE

———— Answer key on page 125. ————

CHRISTMAS WORD SCRAMBLE

Unscramble the following words to form words associated with the birth of Jesus in Bethlehem.

1. nrgame

   _____

2. imga

   _____

3. octlsh

   _____

4. yabb

   _____

5. kyodne

   _____

6. nseagl

   _____

7. eneripnek

   _____

8. smelac

   _____

9. fgsti

   _____

10. isidntg

    _____

11. ceeap

    _____

12. cslkfo

    _____

13. hepse

    _____

14. ehhpressd

    _____

15. dogl

    _____

16. nsrkcnaefein

    _____

17. hymrr

    _____

18. rats

    _____

19. sesiham

    _____

20. astelb

    _____

MORE THEOLOGY TERMS
WORD SEARCH

Words may be horizontal, vertical, or diagonal, forward or backward, and may overlap.

```
E P A T Y C N A R R E N I O E
C F R Z G U Q I M U J F T Q Z
R O R O Z N O I T P M E D E R
E E N E P B N T N E M G D U J
P N C V S I Y V Q E H K R H V
S M O O E U T Y T I R U C E S
S S R I N R R I T I R I P S H
E D T Q T C S R A M H C R N V
N S F E L A I I E T N I O M W
S K A T W E C L O C I I J N O
U D N C S A S I I N T O Y F R
O Y Q R R K R W F A R I N P S
E T B B Z I Q D L I T B O Y H
T I Y V M Q F U S F T I K N I
H N T S C S B I H H C C O R P
G I I F N I M B C W I K N N M
I R N E R I O N W E N P P A Y
R T U T Y Y S H V B L O O D S
```

BLOOD	RESURRECTION	STEWARDSHIP
CONVERSION	RIGHTEOUSNESS	TRIBULATION
INERRANCY	SACRIFICE	TRINITY
JUDGMENT	SANCTIFICATION	UNITY
PROPITIATION	SECURITY	WORSHIP
RECONCILIATION	SIN	
REDEMPTION	SPIRIT	

BOOK OF MATTHEW WHO SAID IT

Chose the person who is speaking in these verses.

1. "I am innocent of this man's blood" (Matthew 27:24).
   a. Judas
   b. Herod
   c. Pilate
   d. Satan

2. "Repent, for the kingdom of heaven has come near" (Matthew 3:2).
   a. John the apostle
   b. John the Baptist
   c. John, relative of the high priest Annas
   d. John the Lesser

3. "You are the Messiah, the son of the living God" (Matthew 16:16).
   a. James
   b. Thomas
   c. Peter
   d. John

4. "Do not be afraid to take Mary home as your wife" (Matthew 1:20).
   a. Zacharias
   b. The angel of the Lord
   c. Joseph's father
   d. John the Baptist

5. "Even if I have to die with you, I will never disown you" (Matthew 26:35).
   a. James
   b. Thomas
   c. Peter
   d. John

6. "Where is the one who has been born king of the Jews?" (Matthew 2:2).
    a. Caesar Augustus
    b. King Herod
    c. Festus
    d. Annas the high priest

7. "If you are the Son of God, tell these stones to become bread." (Matthew 4:3).
    a. Judas
    b. A Pharisee
    c. Satan
    d. A Sadducee

8. "Do not be afraid, for I know that you are looking for Jesus, who was crucified. He is not here; he has risen" (Matthew 28:5).
    a. The gardener
    b. A Roman soldier
    c. Joseph of Arimathea
    d. An angel

9. "Blessed are the meek, for they will inherit the earth" (Matthew 5:5).
    a. Jesus
    b. John the Baptist
    c. John the apostle
    d. Peter

10. "Lord, I do not deserve to have you come under my roof. But just say the word, and my servant will be healed" (Matthew 8:8).
    a. A Pharisee
    b. A centurion
    c. A Roman official
    d. An apostle

—— Answer key on page 126. ——

20/20 VISION

Each of these verses is from chapter 20, verse 20 of an Old Testament book. Can you identify which book each is from?

A. EXODUS
B. NUMBERS
C. DEUTERONOMY

D. 1 SAMUEL
E. 2 KINGS
F. PROVERBS

G. 2 CHRONICLES
H. EZEKIEL

____ 1. "Keep my Sabbaths holy, that they may be a sign between us. Then you will know that I am the LORD your God."

____ 2. "I will shoot three arrows to the side of it, as though I were shooting at a target."

____ 3. "If someone curses their father or mother, their lamp will be snuffed out in pitch darkness."

____ 4. "You may cut down trees that you know are not fruit trees and use them to build siege works until the city at war with you falls."

____ 5. "Moses said to the people, 'Do not be afraid. God has come to test you, so that the fear of God will be with you to keep you from sinning.'"

____ 6. "As for the other events of Hezekiah's reign, all his achievements and how he made the pool and the tunnel by which he brought water into the city, are they not written in the book of the annals?"

____ 7. "[The Edomites] answered, 'You may not pass through.' Then Edom went out against [the Israelites] with a large and powerful army."

____ 8. "Early in the morning they left for the Desert of Tekoa. As they set out, Jehoshaphat stood and said, 'Listen to me, Judah and people of Jerusalem! Have faith in the LORD your God.'"

Answer key on page 126.

WHO WROTE WHAT BOOK?

See if you can match the book of the Bible with the
name of the person who wrote that book.
Some will be used more than once.

A. PAUL   D. SOLOMON   G. UNKNOWN
B. LUKE   E. EZRA   H. JOHN
C. JEREMIAH   F. MOSES

_____ 1. Chronicles

_____ 2. Romans

_____ 3. Hebrews

_____ 4. Revelation

_____ 5. Philemon

_____ 6. Genesis

_____ 7. Ephesians

_____ 8. Ecclesiastes

_____ 9. Acts

_____ 10. Lamentations

MORE HOW'S THAT SPELLED?

Select the proper spelling for each of the
following Bible names.

___ 1.   a. Annanius   b. Annanias   c. Ananias

___ 2.   a. Aquila   b. Aquilla   c. Acquilla

___ 3.   a. Armaggedon   b. Armegedon   c. Armageddon

___ 4.   a. Barthalomew   b. Bartholomew   c. Barthalamu

___ 5.   a. Bathsheba   b. Bethsheba   c. Bethsheeba

___ 6.   a. Eclesiastes   b. Ecclesiastees   c. Ecclesiastes

___ 7.   a. Youphrates   b. Eufrates   c. Euphrates

___ 8.   a. Gethsemane   b. Gethsemene   c. Gethsimane

___ 9.   a. Gamorrah   b. Gomorrah   c. Gamorreh

___ 10.   a. Habbakuk   b. Habakuk   c. Habakkuk

WHO IS SHE?

Give the name of the Bible-times woman
described here.

1. Wife of Jacob and mother of Joseph.

2. Mother of Moses.

3. The only female judge of Israel.

4. She discovered the secret of Samson's strength.

5. Mother of Samuel, the last judge of Israel.

6. A deaconess in the church at Cenchreae.

7. Mother of John the Baptist.

8. The woman who served while her sister listened to Jesus.

9. Widow who remarried and became David's great-grandmother.

10. She heroically dispatched Sisera with a tent peg.

Answer key on page 127.

PROVERBS CROSSWORD

He spoke three thousand proverbs and his songs
numbered a thousand and five. —1 Kings 4:32

Across

1. A father warns that these might try to entice his son (1:10)

4. What goes before destruction (16:18)

5. The name of the Lord is a strong this. (18:10)

8. This calls aloud in the streets (1:20)

10. Number of chapters in proverbs

12. This sharpens iron (27:17)

15. What is exalted by righteousness (14:34)

18. What the people of the city gate bring the woman of Proverbs 31 (31:31)

19. What a wise son brings his father (10:1)

21. This person loves at all times (17:17)

22. What the children of the Proverbs 31 woman call her (31:28)

23. Wrote Proverbs 30 (30:1)

24. What comes after a haughty spirit (16:18)

Down

2. What the Lord determines when man plans his course (16:9)

3. A sluggard is told to observe this insect (6:6)

4. What lazy hands lead a person to be (10:4)

6. What a gentle answer turns away (15:1)

7. A woman of noble character is worth more than these (31:10)

9. He wrote most of the Proverbs

11. Solomon tells his son to eat more of this sweet food (24:14)

13. To have a good one of these is more desirable than great riches (22:1)

14. The woman of Proverbs 31 planted this "out of her earnings" (31:16)

16. This color hair is a "crown of splendor" (16:31)

17. Being led astray by wine or beer is not this (20:1)

20. Wrote Proverbs 31 (31:1)

21. This "of the Lord" is the beginning of wisdom (1:7)

"A" WORDS

Each of these Bible-related words or names
start with the letter "A." Fill in the blank.

A_____   1. The first in an alphabetical list of
Bible names.

A_____   2. A New Testament word that has a
meaning somewhat like the English
word "daddy."

A_____   3. What Jesus made for us when He died
on the cross. It is a covering for our sin.

A_____   4. A country north and east of Israel
that conquered the Northern Kingdom
in 722 BC.

A_____   5. David's son who tried to steal his
throne.

A_____   6. One of the Greek words for love. It
refers to a selfless love.

A_____   7. A perfume that was used by a woman
at Bethany to anoint Jesus.

A_____   8. The first letter of the Greek alphabet.
The last letter is Omega.

A_____   9. The name of a minor prophet who was
also a shepherd.

A_____   10. A selection of religious writings
that do not appear in the Protestant
Bible but that are included in the
Catholic Bible.

GEOGRAPHY LESSON

Provide the answer for each geography-related question.

1. The Bible often uses Beersheba and Dan as north-south border markers for Israel. Identify which is the northern marker and which is the southern marker.

2. When the people of Israel crossed into the Promised Land at the Jordan River under Joshua's leadership, the direction they were going was either east to west or west to east. Chose the correct direction.

3. This body of water runs from the Sea of Galilee to the Dead Sea.

4. Caesarea Philippi is in the northern part of Israel at the foot of this mountain.

5. Of these three locations, this one is on the coast of the Mediterranean Sea: Tekoa, Joppa, Gezer.

6. Choose the larger body of water: Dead Sea or Sea of Galilee.

7. Choose the direction Nazareth is in relation to Bethlehem; it is either north or south.

8. Choose the coast of the Sea of Galilee that the town of Capernaum is located on: north, east, or south.

9. Pick the town that is closer to Jerusalem: Bethany or Bethlehem.

10. Tradition has it that both Paul and Peter were incarcerated in the Mamertine prison. Name the European city where this prison was located.

MIRACLES OF JESUS CROSSWORD

"Jesus of Nazareth was man accredited by God
to you by miracles, wonders and signs, which God did among
you through him." —Acts 2:22

Across

3. Town where Jesus performed His first miracle.

5. Jesus used this many loaves to feed five thousand people.

7. When Jesus walked on water, the disciples first thought they were seeing one of these.

9. Jesus cast the demons from a demon-possessed man into these in the Gadarenes.

10. When Jesus cast demons from a man (Matthew 9), the Pharisees said He did it by the power of the "prince of _____."

12. After Jesus was arrested, he had to reattach this to the servant of the high priest.

15. Jesus was about to heal a boy with an evil spirit, and his father said, "I believe, help my _____."

17. Made the request for Jesus to perform His first miracle.

18. Jesus healed this man's mother-in-law.

19. The number of days Lazarus was in the grave before Jesus raised him.

20. Jesus appeared suddenly in a locked room to prove to this man that He was alive again.

23. The town in which Jesus healed Peter's mother-in-law.

24. The number of loaves Jesus used to feed the four thousand.

Down

1. What the crowd did at Jesus when He said a ruler's daughter was asleep.

2. After Jesus calmed the sea, His disciples said, "Even the wind and the _____ obey Him."

4. Jesus turned water into wine at this event.

6. What the teachers of the law accused Jesus of when He forgave the sins of a paralytic man.

8. After Jesus healed ten men who had leprosy, how many came back to thank Him?

11. When Jesus healed a man in a pool by the Sheep Gate, He got in trouble with the Jews because it was this day.

13. What Jesus revealed to all at His first miracle.

14. The part of Jesus's garment a women who had been bleeding for twelve years touched—and was healed.

16. Jesus marveled at this trait of the centurion after He healed the man's servant.

18. Jesus told the man healed from leprosy (Matthew 8) to first go see the _____.

21. In Luke 9, Jesus's disciples asked about a man: "Who _____ that he was born blind?"

22. After Jesus fed five thousand people, the disciples picked up the remaining food in these.

JERUSALEM:
A CITY WORTH REMEMBERING

Choose the letter of the correct answer.

1. The short word often used to refer to Jerusalem.
    a. Aslan
    b. Zion
    c. Zebu
    d. Cebu
2. Before it was taken by the Israelites under King David, Jerusalem was called this.
    a. Jebus
    b. Zander
    c. Jeru City
    d. Cebus
3. Sometimes Jerusalem is referred to as the "City of . . ." this king.
    a. Saul
    b. Rehoboam
    c. Solomon
    d. David
4. This was the king who built a palace in Jerusalem.
    a. Saul
    b. David
    c. Solomon
    d. Rehoboam
5. This king built the temple in Jerusalem.
    a. Saul
    b. David
    c. Solomon
    d. Rehoboam

6. After the kingdom was divided, the capital of Israel became this city.
    a. Jericho
    b. Gath
    c. Samaria
    d. Beersheba
7. After the kingdom was divided, Jerusalem became the capital of this country.
    a. Syria
    b. Judah
    c. Judea
    d. Hazar
8. In 586 BC, this country destroyed Jerusalem and took its citizens captive.
    a. Babylon
    b. Greece
    c. Egypt
    d. Rome
9. This king allowed Ezra and Nehemiah to return to Jerusalem to rebuild the city and the walls.
    a. Tut
    b. Cyrus
    c. Henry VIII
    d. Ahasuerus
10. In Revelation 21, John said the Holy City would be called this?
    a. Holy Jerusalem
    b. New Jerusalem
    c. Jerusalem of God
    d. Heavenly Jerusalem

THE BOOK OF DANIEL WORD SEARCH

Words may be horizontal, vertical, or diagonal,
forward or backward, and may overlap.

```
W K R E I H T L A E H D V D Q K
H A N D W R I T I N G E X T C V
B U T U C D C Q S T S A E B I N
Z H H E D R Q W Y X A E Q S E L
T G W F R E U S U K R U I B Y W
E S O L E A H S I M F O U Y I C
R I I A W M G P D U N C M S Y X
P H F N T S W X N S H H D R A O
R F O G E N D E B A C O U G J P
E U U L A N Q J D A M S Y P Q V
T R E A Z L U N R L E I R B A G
N N N N M J E D C H C M A R A G
I A Y G H Z A I A Q E M U M O W
S C M U Z H L I C O L E I N A D
N E E A S O R Q F P E U T A T S
O A R G D A I Q H A I N A N A H
I M R E Z S R E G O L O R T S A
L O R A J G P E N O L Y B A B R
```

ABEDNEGO	DREAMS	INTERPRET	STATUE
ASTROLOGERS	FURNACE	LANGUAGE	VISIONS
AZARIAH	GABRIEL	LIONS	WATER
BABYLON	GOAT	MISHAEL	WISDOM
BEASTS	HANANIAH	NEBUCHADNEZZAR	
CYRUS	HANDWRITING	RAM	
DANIEL	HEALTHIER	SHADRACH	

THE PASSOVER OF EXODUS 12 WORD SEARCH

Words may be horizontal, vertical, or diagonal,
forward or backward, and may overlap.

```
S O R D I N A N C E F E R K Y
T F I E B V W K V Y N I G B G
A T F U N O R A A V Q Y R F D
F Z A V X H H E R B S E E E O
F E F Y A Z Y L R E A Y S V O
R O A S T E D F W D B E L T R
N J T F H T A E M H W Y M N F
R E R O E G Y P T T B O S N R
O D E S X M I M R N S O L G A
B O V K J U D G M E N T A I M
T C O B T L H X S T E I D S E
S W S T H U A H D M C S N X S
R T S O G F Q V D L O R A E Y
I B A F I N T N I D C A S K E
F B P H L U H S O T X E P A V
C M A L I F W O A Y S L S O Y
I A Y Z W A L Q Y E M E J L Q
R L W D T B O L A G Y X F C O
A H O U S E H O L D A Y S V O
R T S O G F Q V D L O R A E Y
J F I E B V H Y S S O P G B G
```

AARON	FESTIVAL	JUDGMENT	SANDALS
BELT	FIRSTBORN	LAMB	SIGN
BLOOD	HASTE	MEAT	STAFF
BREAD	HERBS	MOSES	TENTH
CLOAK	HOUSEHOLD	ORDINANCE	TWILIGHT
DOORFRAMES	HYSSOP	PASSOVER	YEAROLD
EGYPT	ISRAEL	ROASTED	YEAST

WHO DID IT?

Choose the letter of the person who
did the action described.

1. Stole items from Ai after Israel had defeated that town.
   - a. Amos
   - b. Asenath
   - c. Achan
   - d. Ananias
2. Took a horse ride at night to inspect the fallen walls of Jerusalem.
   - a. Ezra
   - b. Nehemiah
   - c. David
   - d. Solomon
3. Created a golden calf out of jewelry.
   - a. Aaron
   - b. Miriam
   - c. Balak
   - d. Baruch
4. Was exiled to the island of Patmos.
   - a. Paul
   - b. Barnabas
   - c. John
   - d. Mark
5. Stood on a high platform and read the Law of Moses to the people of Jerusalem after they had returned from exile.
   - a. Joshua
   - b. Nehemiah
   - c. Cyrus
   - d. Ezra

6. Walked on the water of the Sea of Galilee.
    a. Thomas
    b. John
    c. Andrew
    d. Peter
7. Was shipwrecked near the island of Malta.
    a. Barnabas
    b. John Mark
    c. Paul
    d. Cleopas
8. Cut off a part of Saul's robe while in a cave.
    a. Jonathan
    b. David
    c. Absalom
    d. Saul's wife
9. Ate locusts and honey while in the wilderness.
    a. Jesus
    b. Peter
    c. Moses
    d. John the Baptist
10. Escaped to Mount Sinai after he was threatened by Queen Jezebel.
    a. Elisha
    b. Elijah
    c. King Ahab
    d. Gideon

MATTHEW'S GENEALOGY OF JESUS
WORD SEARCH

Words may be horizontal, vertical, or diagonal,
forward or backward, and may overlap.

```
A A M M I N A D A B L E S S E J
P B F H P F A M O N H O A D D U
H H R Z W D F H K U H N K X Z S
S E O A N E P L L M X X R Z H N
A Z O O H E V S A N H N I E A I
W R B B S A A R X T V A A H S A
V O M O P L M K M Z H L S A B B
H N J J M A S I A H T H A I V F
P R D O H G K H A I O C J Y D O
J U N T M A A I E N N A M G I V
C E O B I L S L I Y H S Q S V N
J J H L E O C C R O Z A U U A O
A B E O J E H O R A M D J R D V
A B O W S F T D K Z T Q K G D D
Y H I C M H B T O Z R Z E R E P
K D A H A R A M A O B O H E R
E T S D U J A P V N A H T T A M
L A Y W U D P Z H N O M O L O S
F K T L V J A F A A Q W B N M S
J E C O N I A H P E T A E U I G
V Z A D O K D U H I L E D Q K R
B Z P S O W Y G Z R N E U N A K
```

ABIHUD	ASA	HEZRON	JOSEPH	PEREZ
ABIJAH	AZOR	ISAAC	JOSIAH	RAM
ABRAHAM	BOAZ	JACOB	JOTHAM	REHOBOAM
AHAZ	DAVID	JECONIAH	JUDAH	SHEALTIEL
AKIM	ELEAZAR	JEHORAM	MATTHAN	SOLOMON
AMMINADAB	ELIAKIM	JEHOSHAPHAT	NAHSHON	UZZIAH
AMON	ELIHUD	JESSE	OBED	ZADOK

COUNTRIES IN THE BIBLE
(OTHER THAN ISRAEL) WORD SEARCH

Words may be horizontal, vertical, or diagonal,
forward or backward, and may overlap.

```
O A J N M N A I N O D E C A M
W R D O O J P U N O L Y B A B
G G C P R Y I M O C T I L Y A
L U L T Y D A T L A M M O D E
Z F Z P E G A B S Z I L M U P
E M E A K C O N J E P B D N T
C R E P R V K U M G N X A W Y
E P U B U H B A I Y S S K R O
E I D O T W T T C P M M Z Q A
R X Q J T D A K W T G Q T I M
G I V P U L A A N W N H F P P
K J W J Y D G A I Y B X C K R
S F I G Q Z A V Y P A Y B I L
A P D N L T B H A N O S U P Z
I A A A D O K S O A N I F W N
R W U I M I U N E L I J H X M
Y S Z F N R A T E D P S A T V
S O M O P B E D H S S E R D E
S B D Y E R W I T A E Q R E T
A Z C L C K B O Z M Z K W T P
```

ARABIA	EDOM	ITALY	MACEDONIA
ASSYRIA	EGYPT	JORDAN	MALTA
BABYLON	ETHIOPIA	JUDAH	PERSIA
CRETE	GREECE	LEBANON	SPAIN
CYPRUS	INDIA	LIBYA	TURKEY

Answer key on page 130.

BOOK OF GENESIS CROSSWORD

"In the beginning God . . ." –Genesis 1:1

Across

1. What event led Jacob's sons to have to go to Egypt?

3. First son of Abraham.

4. According to Genesis 2:24, a husband and wife were to become one _____.

7. The people of this city built a tall tower to reach the heavens.

8. Where Joseph was taken after he was sold by his brothers.

10. This brother committed the first murder.

12. Noah found this in the eyes of the Lord (6:8).

13. The wood God told Noah to use to build the ark.

15. The first bird Noah released after the rain stopped.

16. What God sent Abraham to save Isaac's life.

17. Abraham's reaction when God told him he would have a son at age 99.

19. What family prize Jacob and Esau fought over.

20. Son of Jacob who dreamed about his brothers.

Down

2. A man who was called by God to move from Ur to the Promised Land.

3. Sarah and Abraham's son.

5. Nephew of Abraham, he took the good land.

6. What Noah built to honor God after the flood ended.

9. This man's wife wrongly accused Joseph, landing him in prison.

10. The type of promise God made to Noah after the flood.

11. The serpent told Eve she would not do this if she ate the fruit from the tree.

12. Number of days rain fell on the earth during the flood.

14. What God called the "expanse" in 1:8.

16. Jacob and Esau's mother; Isaac's wife.

18. God sent this to tell man-kind that He wouldn't flood the Earth again.

19. What Joseph made his brothers agree would someday be taken to the promised land.

HOW MANY?

In the following biblical situations,
what number is missing?

1. There were _____ cherubim on the Ark of the Covenant.

2. The Israelites marched around Jericho _____ times on the day the walls fell.

3. Jesus was in the wilderness for _____ days before He was tempted.

4. After the flood, the total population of the world was _____ people.

5. The Northern Kingdom of Israel consisted of _____ tribes.

6. Israel spent _____ years in exile in Babylon.

7. In the New Jerusalem of Revelation 21, there will be _____ gates.

8. The fruit of the spirit (Galatians 5:22–23) consists of _____ characteristics.

9. When Moses died, Israel mourned for him for _____ days.

10. When Jesus fed the 5,000, he started with _____ fish and _____ loaves.

—— Answer key on page 131. ——

Words may be horizontal, vertical, or diagonal,
forward or backward, and may overlap.

```
K P U S T F I G U R A T I V E J
C P Y Z E Y R O G E L L A A K G
D O A U T H P K C I T P O N Y S
J I N P G S B G R H I D I O M L
Q Z M C O I T S N O Z W M J G X
C S S M O L E P M N H V Q Z G N
L D E I I R O U I S O P S D Q X
A X L M S N D G G R I C A P K T
C U Q I A E E A E O C L I T H X
I T P Y T N G N N T L S A X E D
T H S G B U T E T C I A U G E M
S E Y O L J R I X R E C C N E L
A O C L W B I G C E H J S E A L
I P N O D F E D Y S I T S O D M
S H A T W E Y O D K Q T E L K H
E A R A M H O M I L E T I C S N
L N R H P L N P T B J P G V Y O
C Y E C Y Y G O L O P Y T D R N
C M N S Y Q A E N H J D A H K A
E T I E J Q M O T I F D U L O C
```

ALLEGORY	ESCHATOLOGY	INERRANCY	MOTIF
APOLOGETICS	EXEGESIS	LEGALISM	SEMANTICS
CANON	FIGURATIVE	LEXICON	SYNOPTIC
CONCORDANCE	HOMILETICS	LITURGY	THEOPHANY
DECALOGUE	IDIOM	MANUSCRIPTS	TYPOLOGY
ECCLESIASTICAL	IMMINENT	METAPHOR	

BOOK OF PSALMS FILL-IN

Complete the following verses by providing
the missing word or words.

1. "_____ is the one who does not walk in step with the wicked" (1:1).

2. "I lie down and _____; I wake up again, because the LORD sustains me" (3:5).

3. "Whoever digs a hole and scoops it out falls into the _____ they have made" (7:15).

4. "LORD, our Lord, how _____ is your name in all the earth" (8:1, 9).

5. "You have made [human beings] a little lower than the _____" (8:5).

6. "The _____ says in his heart, 'There is no God'" (14:1).

7. "Keep me as the _____ of your eye" (17:8).

8. "God is my _____, in whom I take refuge" (18:2).

9. "The _____ declare the glory of God" (19:1).

10. "The law of the LORD is perfect, refreshing the _____" (19:7).

11. "Who may ascend the mountain of the Lord? Who may stand in his holy place? The one who has clean _____ and a _____ heart" (24:3–4).

12. "The LORD is my _____ and my _____, whom shall I fear?" (27:1).

13. "Blessed is the one whose _____ are forgiven" (32:1).

14. "_____ and see that the LORD is good" (34:8).

15. "The eyes of the Lord are on the _____" (34:15).

WHAT LOVE IS

The following thoughts are from 1 Corinthians 13:4–6.
Finish each idea with the word given in that passage.
The first letter of each word is provided.

1. Love is p_____.

2. Love is k_____.

3. It does not e_____.

4. It does not b_____.

5. It is not p_____.

6. It does not d_____ others.

7. It is not s_____-s_____.

8. It is not easily a_____.

9. It keeps no record of w_____.

10. Love does not delight in evil but r_____
    with the truth.

——— Answer key on page 132. ———

MEN OF THE BIBLE WORD SEARCH

Words may be horizontal, vertical, or diagonal,
forward or backward, and may overlap.

```
N M M J J V S J B Z B M A D A
F J O A B K O W W E H T T A M
H P Z O R S C U A B N W K M O
C A D M E K A E I A B D A D S
T U G P I L Q C Y R I Y M N I
B L H G U B N O E D I G J B D
P F E K A L H U K I S T A T Z
B I E P G I M H H Y H J C X U
D P A N X E E C S A P O O X Z
P L B B Y R A P I K B H B N Q
T V R D O L H K K A T N O I S
Z H A D A L E J H H I H N H M
E G H M O Z F A N E W A E C R
Y H A V E W U Z U S R I J A A
X A M H C T I Z X S V M O I M
A I J U N A A C P A Y E S O A
C A N L O J A P B N U R H H A
J S L B N A Q I P A V E U E L
F I O P S C A I N M Q J A J A
M J G I Y G J A M E S F C W B
```

ABRAHAM	HAGGAI	JEHOIACHIN	MALACHI
ADAM	HEROD	JEREMIAH	MANASSEH
AHAB	HEZEKIAH	JOB	MARK
AMOS	ISAAC	JOHN	MATTHEW
BALAAM	ISAIAH	JOSEPH	PAUL
CAIN	JACOB	JOSHUA	
GIDEON	JAMES	LUKE	

Words may be horizontal, vertical, or diagonal,
forward or backward, and may overlap.

```
O N F I A E R P P L E U M A S
G E A C C S H A I R A H C E Z
Z H G T X R A L Q A L I U Q A
Z E R U C L X P B Y V Q P Y U
W M I G D P J E H W E R D N A
B I P W X C D S N S U R I A J
E A P X K N O J U O R V M T Y
O H A B E L A C L R M E L A X
X H P G I Z J V P W A O N N U
E A O F A A R W Q C R Z L B W
L O Z O C M E U Y Z E O A O A
E N B O R V S A M S O N I L S
B Z B T A D S E S O M J I O I
A H A L E S U H T E M M T V P
B M U Z Z I A H H A E I J E C
B J R N O E M I S T Y H T H L
U E L I J A H B A O H E Z Q U
R A P O G Z Z L M W R L U A S
E K C I E L I S H A S L E B A
Z X K B W P P E L K A N A H X
```

ABEDNEGO	CALEB	MOSES	SIMEON
ABEL	ELIJAH	NEHEMIAH	SOLOMON
ABNER	ELISHA	NOAH	UZZIAH
AGRIPPA	ELKANAH	PETER	ZECHARIAH
ANDREW	JACOB	PILATE	ZERUBBABEL
AQUILA	JAIRUS	SAMSON	
ASAPH	LAZARUS	SAMUEL	
BOAZ	METHUSELAH	SAUL	

—— *Answer key on page 133.* ——

LIFE OF JESUS CROSSWORD

She will give birth to a son, and you are to give him the name Jesus, because he will save his people from their sins.
—Matthew 1:21

Across

2. At one time, Jesus told Peter to look in one of these to find tax money.

3. Where Mary and Joseph found their son after they discovered he was not in their traveling entourage home from Jerusalem.

5. The meal Jesus fixed for Peter on the beach after the resurrection.

6. At the transfiguration, who joined Jesus and Moses?

7. At least twice the Pharisees attributed Jesus's miracles to these.

9. The Pharisees criticized Jesus because His disciples picked kernels of this on the Sabbath.

11. Jesus's first disciples: Andrew and _____.

13. As He dined with His disciples, Jesus pointed out that this man would betray Him.

15. What word did the crowds shout to Jesus on Palm Sunday?

16. The man who offered his tomb for Jesus's burial.

17. The man who answered correctly when Jesus asked, "Who do people say I am?"

18. What was Simon of Cyrene ordered to carry for Jesus?

Down

1. Who was the man whose sons wanted to sit with Jesus in the kingdom?

2. Jesus cried out on the cross, "Why have you _____ me?"

4. Name of the tax collector who believed in Jesus.

7. After the disciples and Jesus were at Caesarea Philippi, He told them He was going to Jerusalem to do this.

8. When Jesus gave the greatest commandment, He said to love God and love your _____.

10. Peter denied Jesus three times before he heard this creature.

12. The first name we hear Jesus say aloud after His resurrection.

14. Who helped Jesus after the temptation?

16. As Jesus and His disciples were leaving this city, Jesus healed two blind men sitting by the roadside.

BIBLE-TIME PROFESSIONS
WORD SCRAMBLE

Unscramble the following letters to form words associated with jobs and professions in the times of the Bible.

1. rekba _____

2. trubel _____

3. hensarifm _____

4. enurth _____

5. nprreacte _____

6. hhpedres _____

7. emarfr _____

8. gikn _____

9. nevgroor _____

10. onrncieut _____

11. mcaorenmd _____

12. ordlise _____

13. brecis _____

14. tlmgiosdh _____

15. anmteretk _____

16. arbib _____

17. sieptr _____

18. petrpho _____

19. arehtec _____

20. peeeninkr _____

——— *Answer key on page 134.* ———

HOLY SPIRIT FILL-IN

Fill in the blanks in these statements about the Holy Spirit.
The first letter of each fill-in is provided.

1. The Holy Spirit fell on the Christians on the Day of
   P_____.

2. The b_____ is the temple of the Holy Spirit,
   according to 1 Corinthians 6:19.

3. Jesus told the disciples He would send "another
   a_____" in John 14:16.

4. After Jesus's baptism, the Holy Spirit descended on
   Jesus like a d_____.

5. In Ephesians 4:30, Paul said believers should not
   g_____ the Holy Spirit.

6. Love, joy, peace, forbearance, and kindness are called
   the f_____ of the Spirit.

7. Romans 8:26 says the Holy Spirit helps us in our
   w_____.

8. First Corinthians 2:10 says, "The Spirit searches all
   things, even the d_____ things of God.

9. Ephesians 5:18 says, "Do not get drunk with wine, . . .
   instead, be f_____ with the Holy Spirit."

10. Paul said, "Do not q_____ the Spirit"
    (1 Thessalonians 5:19).

Answer key on page 134.

TABERNACLE
WORD SEARCH

Words may be horizontal, vertical, or diagonal,
forward or backward, and may overlap.

```
C T R U O C Y R A U T C N A S
E R Z V I V D N A T S P M A L
D L S N R A T L A T S E I R P
A V H A L V Y T A N R T E Q G
R C O T Z X A M G R N U G L C
G U W L D C Y O K E K A O V H
D R B K N L B N M V W R M E E
W T R W I X O E O B Y J F I R
E A E L A Y N G N U J D E L U
L I A N N O L I N E N L Z N B
L N D I T E M E K D C K U V I
I G O A G W X G E A S N M C M
N P T P Q D B S N T I Y N T L
G T A B L E N R E S S N I K S
E O Y E I E E L A A I C A C A
D D I H C B B B G X B W L W K
G S J N A A E C A L P Y L O H
H V I T T G S G N I R E F F O
R T O T Z X A M G R N U G L C
I G O D E N E V A E L N U C M
```

ACACIA	COURT	LAMPSTAND	SKINS
ALTAR	CURTAIN	LINEN	TABERNACLE
ARK	DWELLING	MANNA	TABLE
ATONEMENT	GLORY	OFFERINGS	TABLETS
BASIN	GOLD	PRIEST	TENT
CEDAR	HOLY PLACE	SANCTUARY	UNLEAVENED
CHERUBIM	INCENSE	SHOWBREAD	VEIL

CITIES AND TOWNS OF THE BIBLE
WORD SEARCH

Words may be horizontal, vertical, or diagonal,
forward or backward, and may overlap.

```
A H S I H C A L F C G H S E H
B R B D D U W F S H S E D E K
F L E H T E B K A B G E Y E J
N G I B E O N F M N A H T O D
O I T D D K J A A R Z O P S J
L E J A H U M R R M A P U E L
E W C E S B P C I G A S R D M
K L K A Z H P K A M W I N Y T
H T E W P R I E H N C X D B P
S J E H G E E L X H A F N E K
A A E K A U R E O N O A N T G
N S C R O Z K N L H Z K A H A
G H H M U A O R A A R D J L H
A D O Y D S B R R U I G O E E
L O R N G C A E W A M U D H B
K D A A Y U T L S M L M D E R
I F Z H S H C H E E C N I M O
Z Q I T Q J T N J M N N G N N
R R N E R E S H M E H C E H S
I O Q B B E M M A U S D M Z X
```

ASHDOD	CAPERNAUM	HEBRON	MEGIDDO
ASHKELON	CHORAZIN	JERICHO	NAZARETH
BETHANY	DOTHAN	JERUSALEM	SAMARIA
BETHEL	EMMAUS	JEZREEL	SHECHEM
BETHLEHEM	GAZA	JOPPA	SHILOH
BETHSAIDA	GIBEON	KEDESH	TEKOA
CANA	HAZOR	LACHISH	ZIKLAG

Answer key on page 135.

MIRACLES CROSSWORD

You are the God who performs miracles;
you display your power among the peoples. —Psalm 77:14

Across

2. What did the magi see that directed them to find Jesus?

4. Commander of an army who was healed after reluctantly bathing in the Jordan River

6. River that opened up so Elisha and Elijah could cross it

8. He had a donkey that spoke to him

9. This Old Testament woman had a baby when she was ninety years old

10. Burning object that got Moses's attention

14. When the ark of the covenant was in the room of an idol named Dagon, the idol did this

16. Gideon set out this on the ground—and it was wet where it should have been dry

18. Disease King Uzziah contracted after he desecrated the temple

19. He was miraculously saved from Sodom and Gomorrah

20. Ordinary implement of Aaron's that budded and grew almonds

Down

1. When Shadrach, Meshech, and Abednego survived the fiery furnace (a pretty good miracle on its own), Nebuchanezzar saw this in the furnace

3. This fed Elijah when he was hiding in the Kerith Ravine

5. Body of water that opened up so the Israelites could escape the Egyptian army

6. Prophet who miraculously survived being swallowed by a large fish

7. Two of these attacked the young men who mocked Elisha

8. Where God intervened and caused people to speak different languages

11. How the water of Marah tasted after Moses threw a piece of wood into the water

12. This prophet's bones brought a man to life

13. A bronze object that healed snake-bitten Israelites

15. The country where God sent the plague of frogs

16. What God sent onto the altars of Mount Carmel in Elijah's battle with Baal's worshipers

17. It guided the Israelites in the daytime while they were in the desert

21. What miraculously multiplied for Elisha so a mom did not lose her boys to creditors

WEIGHTS AND MEASURES
WORD SEARCH

Words may be horizontal, vertical, or diagonal,
forward or backward, and may overlap.

```
M K L K M V Q R Q U A N I M
B C T N U R L L Q A I X X M
D U A H T D A E R B D N A H
H B L E X W B F Z Y H A E S
S I E D R A V J H N U M T M
A T N J Y R T U E Y B A K Z
R L T G K U C X W A D J R C
E C E V U B J C I T W N Q
J L N T I M Y Y A P N W M Y
U O W S H H R R E M O H Q P
E P H A H E Y E H Z B F C D
S M S N O E K H M C R J Z K
C A H H S E K X B O G W M A
H Y C D U H C E P K T O F S
I S M Y A N B Q L V H Z E P
N J E R Q D F V J T T G N A
J S E T T N S E A Z L E O N
W G F L B C G F H J L R S L
```

CAB	HANDBREADTH	MINA	STADIA
CUBIT	HIN	OMER	TALENT
EPHAH	HOMER	SEAH	
FATHOM	LETHEK	SHEKEL	
GERAH	LOG	SPAN	

PLANTS OF THE BIBLE WORD SEARCH

Words may be horizontal, vertical, or diagonal,
forward or backward, and may overlap.

```
U N A C A C I A B Y E L R A B
L D E E R Q F J E L B M A R B
P I U H U E E N I V E P A R G
I P S P I C E S Y N B D S R S
S L A D U L O T U S J T N I M
T Z G A R L I C L Y O P F O Z
A U Y T E T A N A R G E M O P
C A J A D S P W P O P L A R T
H P U E N D Y O Z O Q D L I I
I P S H A H Y O A H N K M T T
O L L W I C K C R A V B R X E
F E I O R C F O G W E E E O L
X N T E O M J T J R B M B Q L
M O N R C A A A P M U L E G I
Q R E O P L G E U S I X F X M
Z F L M O O C C T L S N A E B
P F M A S E U A Y L Y M D L S
Y A P C S C R N O M A N N I C
K S Z Y Y D S U C O R C A P N
Q Z Y S H S Q J C D N O M L A
```

ACACIA	CORIANDER	LOTUS	SAFFRON
ALMOND	CROCUS	MILLET	SPICES
ALOE	CUCUMBER	MINT	SYCAMORE
APPLE	GARLIC	MUSTARD	TIMBER
BARLEY	GRAPEVINE	PISTACHIO	WHEAT
BEANS	HYSSOP	POMEGRANATE	
BRAMBLE	LENTILS	POPLAR	
CINNAMON	LILY	REED	

ANGEL FACTS

Select the best answer from the
four provided.

1. One of these is not among the purposes of angels.
   a. glorify God
   b. fly around in heaven
   c. help people
   d. worship God

2. According to Scripture's record, in one of these events angels were not a part of it.
   a. the events surrounding Jesus's birth
   b. the flood
   c. Jonah's journey to Nineveh
   d. the temptation of Jesus

3. Of the following traits, only one is true of angels. Select that trait.
   a. They are omnipresent.
   b. They are innumerable.
   c. They are omniscient.
   d. They are omnipotent.

4. Choose the one traits angels do not share with humans.
   a. They can marry.
   b. They have intelligence.
   c. They show joy.
   d. They have a will.

5. One of these things is not true of angels. Select that trait.
   a. They are spirit beings.
   b. They are to be worshiped.
   c. They have a free will.
   d. They report directly to God.

6. The word "angel" means . . .
   a. visitor
   b. messenger
   c. winged wonder
   d. deliverer
7. This gospel mentions the name of Gabriel, who appeared to Mary.
   a. Matthew
   b. Mark
   c. Luke
   d. John
8. Pick the one activity an angel did not perform (as far as recorded in Scripture) during the week of Jesus's crucifixion and resurrection.
   a. rolled away the stone in front of Jesus's tomb
   b. announced His resurrection
   c. folded his grave clothes in the tomb
   d. ministered to Jesus in Gethsemane
9. This book of the Bible mentions the word *angel* or *angels* the most times.
   a. Psalms
   b. Matthew
   c. Hebrews
   d. Revelation
10. Pick the two items that are not true.
    a. Angels are created beings separate from humans.
    b. Angels are humans who have died and gone to heaven.
    c. Angels have been known to rebel against God.
    d. Angels look a lot like Precious Moments figurines.

Answer key on page 137.

WORDS ABOUT GOD
WORD SCRAMBLE

Unscramble the following words that describe or characterize God.

1. lguorsio   _____

2. rtoeacr   _____

3. tlrenea   _____

4. uhialfft   _____

5. violgn   _____

6. ratfeh   _____

7. drgwenoelkofe   _____

8. odog   _____

9. ragiscou   _____

10. sisohlen   _____

11. thlig   _____

12. jiestacm   _____

13. etabimlum   _____

14. pratilmai   _____

15. siroepenhbiencml   _____

16. pedntenedni   _____

17. ftininei   _____

18. beisnvlii   _____

19. eolsjau   _____

20. gudje   _____

"E" BIBLE NAMES WORD SEARCH

Words may be horizontal, vertical, or diagonal,
forward or backward, and may overlap.

```
I N D D X Z C P U R N A H T E
Q K X X B E Z E K I E L L I V
H F W Q X I T Y P X C R T K E
C V S F L E Z Y H A N A K L E
O K Z U Z A X I M I K A I L E
N A S R H E E H U D H Y Q Z C
E V A P V C L T Q E P N E B B
R G I V Z W Y E T U L Q R L E
K L J B S Y G T A H O I G P F
E R I G K D X K U Z D G A L S
R P E S T H E R D E A P E S B
E L A F S Q O C N H H R U A E
Z A Z M A H L K T R A C E L S
E B I N V T E E O S M L I O H
N E Q F C L B D T X I J G H A
E H U G E A I U Y S A U M R N
B S H M Z T S U H H R S J M N
E I I I U Q A A B O H B A N D
D L L S N S K L Z N P L D Q T
E E E H E E I P X Y E K R B O
Q K X X B E Z E K I E L L I V
E V A P V C L T Q E P N E B B
```

EBENEZER	ELIJAH	ENOCH	ETHAN
EHUD	ELIMELEK	EPAPHRODITUS	EUTYCHUS
ELAM	ELIPHAZ	EPHRAIM	EVE
ELEAZAR	ELISHA	ERASTUS	EZEKIEL
ELI	ELISHEBA	ESAU	EZRA
ELIAKIM	ELIZABETH	ESHAN	
ELIHU	ELKANAH	ESTHER	

"J" BIBLE NAMES WORD SEARCH

Words may be horizontal, vertical, or diagonal,
forward or backward, and may overlap.

```
B S E M A J I H A I M E R E J I
T A J E S U S E K M B S L E A J
J O N A T H A N H G J T C Y P G
Y J P B Q U W O B T K O G S M J
M O S B E H Q U B D E T A L A W
L S X S V E E O K K Z H J S O J
R E B U Y J C E B V U E P A H U
H P D J O A M A N Q H H I A N D
S H Z U J Z Y R B O J L V V J A
Z I G H J M V I S X U Q O J S H
J F F N N G R H F J Z N U E W I
B O E B L G A A N N A O J H G Y
J Y N E S P K Z O L I R R O K H
G O D A H W A J L W B G Y R N M
V I E A H U O A M A R O J A F I
H E T L H H A I R J A I R M F K
A A W S N B H X J R J E S S E A
M R O Y B A J E R O B O A M Q I
I J S U I O R Z R H T I D U J O
M C R S S E K N E J U D A S W H
E E O W N I H C I O H E J B J E
J J X C Q S U I R A J A G W S J
```

JACOB	JEHORAM	JESUS	JORAM
JAEL	JEHOSHAPHAT	JOANNA	JOSEPH
JAIR	JEHU	JOASH	JOSHUA
JAMES	JEMIMAH	JOB	JOSIAH
JAPHETH	JEREMIAH	JOEL	JUDAH
JARIUS	JEROBOAM	JOHN	JUDAS
JEHOIACHIN	JERUBBAAL	JONAH	JUDE
JEHOIAKIM	JESSE	JONATHAN	JUDITH

PARABLES OF JESUS WORD SCRAMBLE

First, unscramble the words, which each relate to a parable of Jesus. Then use the highlighted letters to fill in the blanks after the puzzle. You will put those highlighted letters in the proper order to define the word parable.

1. enjroyu   ___ ___ ___ ___ ___ ___ ___

2. sbteord   ___ ___ ___ ___ ___ ___ ___

3. wreso   ___ ___ ___ ___ ___

4. erats   ___ ___ ___ ___ ___

5. drsumta   ___ ___ ___ ___ ___ ___ ___

6. ealnev   ___ ___ ___ ___ ___ ___

7. plam   ___ ___ ___ ___

8. gnarted   ___ ___ ___ ___ ___ ___ ___

9. retasreu   ___ ___ ___ ___ ___ ___ ___ ___

10. newi   ___ ___ ___ ___

11. vathers   ___ ___ ___ ___ ___ ___ ___

12. anitmarsa   ___ ___ ___ ___ ___ ___ ___ ___ ___

13. erhspdeh   ___ ___ ___ ___ ___ ___ ___ ___

14. eagt   ___ ___ ___ ___

15. dinewdg   ___ ___ ___ ___ ___ ___ ___

16. werot   ___ ___ ___ ___ ___

17. inco   ___ ___ ___ ___

18. ligradpo   ___ ___ ___ ___ ___ ___ ___ ___

19. daryeniv   ___ ___ ___ ___ ___ ___ ___ ___

20. giinrsv   ___ ___ ___ ___ ___ ___ ___

___ ___ ___ ___ ___ ___ ___ ___ ___ ___ ___ ___ ___ ___

___ ___ ___ ___ ___ ___ ___ ___ ___ ___ ___ ___ ___ ___ ___ ___

___ ___ ___ ___ ___ ___ ___ .

BOOK OF PHILIPPIANS CROSSWORD

Whatever happens, conduct yourselves in a manner worthy of the gospel of Christ. —Philippians 1:27

Across

2. In 4:5, where did Paul say the Lord is?

3. When Paul listed things that are excellent and praiseworthy that believers should think about, his first was "whatever is" this.

6. The book of Philippians was written to the people of this city.

8. For the "enemies of the cross," their god is this part of the body.

9. Paul said that the things that happened to him served to advance this.

10. Twice in Philippians 4:4, Paul said believers should always do this in the Lord.

14. The true citizenship of the Christian is found in this place.

15. Whose interests did Paul say we should look out for instead of our own?

16. Paul said he desired to depart the earth and be with this person.

17. Apparently, Euodia and Syntyche were arguing. Instead, Paul wanted them to have the same this.

20. The animal Paul used to describe "mutilators of the flesh."

22. The person Paul wanted to send to the people to whom he was writing.

Down

1. Philippians was written to the _____ in Jesus Christ.

2. Paul told the church God would meet all of these for them.

4. Philippians was a letter. This is another word for "letter."

5. How Paul told his "dear friends" to stand.

7. Someday, at the name of Jesus every knee will do this before Him.

8. What Jesus took the nature of when He left heaven and came to earth.

11. In Philippians 4:11, Paul says he has learned to be this "whatever the circumstances."

12. Paul said it is important to "_____ on" toward the goal.

13. The restraining device Paul was in when he wrote Philippians.

18. Paul mentioned Epaphroditus, who almost did this.

19. Where Paul was when he wrote this letter to the Philippians.

21. Finish this: "For to me to live is Christ and to die is _____." (1:21).

PRECIOUS STONES OF THE BIBLE
WORD SEARCH

Words may be horizontal, vertical, or diagonal,
forward or backward, and may overlap.

```
C A R N E L I A N V Z C M Z S
Z K B Y P U X X B D T I D K A
A T D N W I Q Y P L R G Y G E
P C E Q C C P N Y A P U A O D
O T L P P A C O P T A T B I E
T R L E S E R S Z E E P A Y R
U J I A S N T B D M D M K V I
D E U R C V Q I U E O W R P H
C D M L B Y C H L N R N E D P
Y S Q S G H N K D O C U G L P
Y J A S P E R O W Q S L G L A
A M E T H Y S T D B Q Y E I S
O F T N A M A D A E E J R G L
G S U R F E S D H G C R M H P
Z I E M G U I Y Y T C L Y M C
E Q A V I R H G R L N V A L V
C S N D E V S L A B E I F H D
G Z R B L A R O C L T B C U C
T A M L S A R D O N Y X E A V
S A B V V N C R Y S T A L F J
```

ADAMANT	CARBUNCLE	DIAMOND	SAPPHIRE
AGATE	CARNELIAN	JASPER	SARDIUS
AMBER	CHALCEDONY	LIGURE	SARDONYX
AMETHYST	CHRYSOLITE	ONYX	TOPAZ
BDELLIUM	CORAL	PEARLS	
BERYL	CRYSTAL	RUBY	

Note: These stones are not all mentioned in the New International Version. Some of these are terms used in the King James Version and the New King James Version.

TREES OF THE BIBLE
WORD SEARCH

Words may be horizontal, vertical, or diagonal,
forward or backward, and may overlap.

```
S V A L O E S J O L R O M C P
Q Y P L T N E X L B O X Y I Z
W G C J H L R R I F F P N M W
A I I A P A U O V Q R E A K B
U L L P M C Z G E E V Z A D G
Z D A L I O U E S P W G S O C
T Y U Q O N R S L S B R P E F
N L E X E W Q E D X I H D I M
D Z J C P X S R V K E A G Q D
W Z J I U G J Z J R R B M J K
X M U N H O K A A S H A R B Z
Y E N N H M A N D N O M L A I
O G I A T T H K O V R G F Y V
Y S P M N M N D A T E R N R V
O G E O R R Y I M Q U O D R A
C Q R N X M Q R B I B O K E I
W U T L Z P L M T E D B C B C
M I G P O P L A R L R C S L A
C H E S T N U T P M E E N U C
P O M E G R A N A T E X T M A
Q Y P E X L B O X Y I Z N M W
N L E Q E D X I H D I M A K B
```

ACACIA	CHESTNUT	GOPHER	PALM
ALMOND	CINNAMON	HAZEL	PINE
ALOES	CYPRESS	JUNIPER	POMEGRANATE
APPLE	DATE	MULBERRY	POPLAR
ASH	EBONY	MYRTLE	SYCAMORE
BOX	FIG	OAK	TEREBINTH
CEDAR	FRUIT	OLIVE	WILLOW

IN THE BIBLE OR NOT?

Look at each of the following sayings and write
"yes" or "no" to indicate if you think it is actually
a quote from the Bible.

____ 1. "All hard work brings a profit."

____ 2. "Cleanliness is next to godliness."

____ 3. "God works in mysterious ways, His wonders to
perform."

____ 4. "Better to live in a desert than with a quarrelsome
and nagging wife."

____ 5. "The wings of the ostrich flap joyfully."

____ 6. "God will not give you more than you can handle."

____ 7. "God helps those who help themselves."

____ 8. "How good and pleasant it is when God's people
live together in unity."

____ 9. "Hate the sin, love the sinner."

____ 10. "I have escaped only by the skin of my teeth."

Answer key on page 141.

WORDS ASSOCIATED WITH JESUS
WORD SEARCH

Words may be horizontal, vertical, or diagonal,
forward or backward, and may overlap.

```
R S B U B S S E L N I S J B U C
L E M E L A S U R E J V D B O O
F Q D Z T L C W M E I E X M S S
O E B E A H D G S P Y I P M A I
W T R Y M O L P C A C A H C O N
X E L S A P I E R R S J R O A C
Z R M F H E T T H S E I T B L A
C N U R D E E I I E F A S U P R
G A A M E B P O O I M N T A H N
N L N K I I N H C N O T S O A A
I W R Q T O U E E I K C U Z R T
L H E F Y Q O T X R E S A S L I
A O P L U Q E I Q N D R N B O O
E L A X S A F X S A E R Y M H N
H Y C N C I U I L T Q Q R A U X
Z V Y H C Q O M H E Z C Q L M N
X S E U S N Q L K C V M Y L A N
G R R R E S U R R E C T I O N V
I C I R V G J G N I H C A E R P
P I M M A N U E L A G D A G V G
P I P P Y I U Z C U U T A L T G
R N X I L K A B U S Y L O J O N
```

ALPHA	CRUCIFIXION	INCARNATION	RESURRECTION
ASCENSION	DEITY	JERUSALEM	SACRIFICE
BETHLEHEM	ETERNAL	KING	SHEPHERD
BETRAYED	HEALING	LAMB	SINLESS
CAPERNAUM	HOLY	NAZARETH	TEACHER
COMPASSION	HUMAN	PREACHING	
CREATOR	IMMANUEL	REDEMPTION	

WHERE'S THAT QUOTE?

Pick the book of the Bible that contains
the quoted verse.

1. "A wise son brings joy to his father."
    a. Ecclesiastes
    b. Ephesians
    c. Proverbs
    d. Psalms

2. "All have sinned and fall short of the glory of God."
    a. Acts
    b. Romans
    c. Ephesians
    d. Philippians

3. "How good and pleasant it is when God's people live together in unity!"
    a. Psalms
    b. Titus
    c. Colossians
    d. Hebrews

4. "Trust in the Lord with all your heart and lean not on your own understanding."
    a. James
    b. Philippians
    c. Psalms
    d. Proverbs

5. "Do not conform to the pattern of this world, but be transformed by the renewing of your mind."
    a. Colossians
    b. 1 Corinthians
    c. Acts
    d. Romans

6. "Go and make disciples of all nations, baptizing them in the name of the Father and of the Son and of the Holy Spirit."
    a. Luke
    b. Mark
    c. Matthew
    d. John

7. "All Scripture is God-breathed and is useful for teaching, rebuking, correcting and training in righteousness."
    a. 1 Timothy
    b. 2 Timothy
    c. Titus
    d. 1 Thessalonians

8. "For we are God's handiwork, created in Christ Jesus to do good works, which God prepared in advance for us to do."
    a. Ephesians
    b. Colossians
    c. Galatians
    d. Philippians

9. "'For I know the plans I have for you,' declares the LORD, 'plans to prosper you and not to harm you, plans to give you hope and a future.'"
    a. Daniel
    b. Joshua
    c. Isaiah
    d. Jeremiah

10. "Seek first his kingdom and his righteousness, and all these things will be given to you as well."
    a. Matthew
    b. Acts
    c. Hebrews
    d. James

BIBLE FIRSTS CROSSWORD

The Son is the image of the invisible God,
the firstborn over all creation. —Colossians 1:15

Across

4. First specific living creatures mentioned at creation

6. He conducted the first recorded business transaction (buying a burial plot for his wife)

7. First land animal mentioned at creation

8. The first mother of twins mentioned

12. First person in Scripture to go to heaven without dying

13. Told the Bible's first riddle

15. First living thing that left the ark and didn't return

17. First people to visit Jesus after His birth

20. Winner of the first beauty pageant mentioned in Scripture

21. God's first command: "Let there be _____"

22. He preached the first gospel sermon

23. Book of Bible other than Genesis that starts, "In the beginning"

Down

1. The first keeper of flocks in Scripture

2. Had first recorded dream in the Bible

3. First person to see the risen Lord

5. She baked the first cake recorded in Scripture

7. The first murderer in the Bible

9. Result of first plague suffered by Egyptians

10. At his death, physicians were first mentioned

11. Fruit of first garden planted after the ark landed

14. First person we are told about who got drunk

16. Event where Jesus did His first recorded miracle

18. First map direction used in Scripture

19. First color mentioned in the Bible

20. First left-handed person recorded

22. The first person said to have a disease

JESUS QUOTE FILL-IN

Fill in the missing word or words in the
following quotes of Jesus.

1. "Man shall not live on _____ alone." Matthew 4:4.

2. "Follow Me, and I will send you out to _____ for
_____." Matthew 4:19

3. "Blessed are the _____, for they will inherit the
earth." Matthew 5:5

4. "You are the _____ of the earth." Matthew 5:13

5. "Love your _____ and pray for those who
persecute you." Matthew 5:44

6. "Store up for yourselves treasures in _____."
Matthew 6:20

7. "The harvest is _____ but the workers are few."
Matthew 9:37

8. "The _____ was made for man, not man for
the _____." Mark 2:27

9. "Whoever does God's _____ is my brother and
sister and mother." Mark 3:35

10. "Let the _____ _____ come to me, and
do not hinder them." Mark 10:14

Answer key on page 142.

"M" BIBLICAL NAMES AND PLACES

Words may be horizontal, vertical, or diagonal,
forward or backward, and may overlap.

```
M A R T H A H A L E S U H T E M
I B T T T H M A T T H E W N R B
D E R R D L A M E I L A H C I M
I M L A C Q E R H H A B I R E M
A N O T K G T C A Z O L O T I N
N M Y R I R A Y I M U G T G F E
B H V D I L A I D L E A H C I M
D P D J A A D D M A G D A L A V
X O B M F G H B F C A I B Q J M
O P J M A N A S S E H M W T E G
M E L C H I Z E D E K V W S X M
H M M A M R E S I S C Z H Q I R
Z E Q Z N R J R X K I A Y C F S
G L H D Q Z L V A M C H H R S K
X C A S J P B I I H N A P A A P
K H L Y Q V N R X S H H I M X M
W I E V F O I Q U S U H Q R E M
Y A P F D A Y H E G T T Z H O M
K H H E M T C Y O T A N E A B Y
R X C P Q L B G A U K N B L O O
A A A B A J A M L V H W B T I C
M I M M G M V N H T K S O B G M
```

MACEDONIA	MARAH	MELCHIZEDEK	MIDIAN
MACHPELAH	MARK	MEMPHIS	MILETUS
MAGDALA	MARTHA	MERIBAH	MIRIAM
MAGOG	MARY	MESHACH	MOAB
MALACHI	MATTHEW	METHUSELAH	MORIAH
MALCHUS	MATTHIAS	MICHAEL	
MAMRE	MEGIDDO	MICHAH*	
MANASSEH	MELCHIAH	MICHAL	

* KJV spelling

Answer key on page 143.

BIBLICAL PROPHETS WORD SEARCH

Words may be horizontal, vertical, or diagonal,
forward or backward, and may overlap.

```
E  Z  E  K  I  E  L  O  A  H  S  I  L  E  S
W  M  J  V  M  E  D  N  B  H  O  S  E  A  I
E  L  I  J  A  H  N  A  S  E  C  L  K  H  N
K  V  J  A  P  T  X  I  D  W  D  J  E  A  M
R  N  H  B  X  R  U  D  L  Y  T  U  H  O  V
E  K  A  X  Z  Z  N  Q  I  J  K  U  L  Z  J
O  Q  I  L  Q  M  V  N  K  U  M  N  Z  N  O
A  G  A  H  H  A  C  I  M  L  E  I  N  A  D
H  I  S  Y  Q  K  L  X  Z  Z  B  C  K  L  A
B  H  I  C  P  Z  E  C  H  A  R  I  A  H  J
I  C  E  E  E  D  Q  M  I  A  Y  S  W  E  R
Y  A  X  U  C  O  H  V  E  Y  H  O  R  W  J
G  L  Q  X  K  A  G  K  H  A  C  E  F  O  K
P  A  D  K  D  U  A  V  I  A  M  W  N  V  F
P  M  W  L  X  V  K  N  K  I  I  A  P  I  M
C  L  U  Q  U  D  A  K  A  V  H  D  A  N  M
Z  H  Q  Y  D  H  O  H  A  I  B  G  A  P  R
Q  X  N  U  P  Z  U  B  R  B  G  Q  R  B  W
C  E  G  E  S  O  M  A  T  A  A  A  F  N  O
M  G  Z  U  M  G  G  C  H  M  Q  H  G  Y  R
```

AMOS	HABAKKUK	JEREMIAH	NAHUM
DANIEL	HAGGAI	JOEL	OBADIAH
ELIJAH	HOSEA	JONAH	OBED
ELISHA	HULDAH	MALACHI	ZECHARIAH
EZEKIEL	ISAIAH	MICAH	ZEPHANIAH

—— *Answer key on page 143.* ——

WORD SEARCH
& ACTIVITY BOOK

SOLUTIONS
AND
ANSWERS

Basic Bible Facts

1. 66
2. 39
3. 27
4. Psalms
5. Hebrews
6. Genesis
7. Matthew, Mark, Luke, John
8. Luke
9. Revelation
10. Proverbs, Ecclesiastes, Song of Songs

Women of the Bible Word Search

More Basic Bible Facts

1. Torah or Pentateuch
2. Moses
3. David
4. Hebrew
5. Greek
6. Jeremiah and Psalms would both be acceptable answers. It depends on who is doing the counting—and whether you are

counting Hebrew words or English words. In the King James Version, Psalms has about fifty more words: both in the 42,700 range.

Note: In the original manuscripts, 1 and 2 Samuel, 1 and 2 Kings, and 1 and 2 Chronicles were together as one book. Each pair would be longer than Jeremiah or Psalms if they had been kept together.

7. 3 John (220 words)
8. Hebrews
9. The Dead Sea Scrolls
10. False. Those were added by translators about eight hundred years ago.

The Exodus Word Search

Who Said It?

1. H (Ruth 1:16)
2. G (Philippians 4:13)
3. F (Genesis 5:1; 10:3).
   They were quoting God when they said this.
4. E (Genesis 50:20 NKJV)
5. A (Psalm 23:1)
6. I (Ecclesiastes 12:1)
7. G (1 Corinthians 13:4)
8. B (Isaiah 40:31)
9. C (James 5:16)
10. D (Matthew 12:28)

King David Crossword

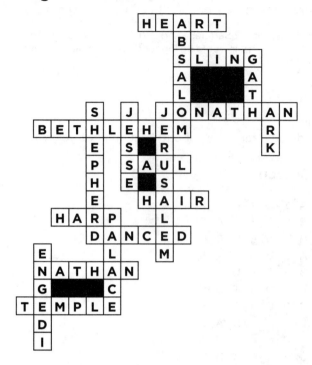

Wonders of Nature in Job 38 Word Search

Old Testament Chronology

A. 16   E. 10   I. 3   M. 6
B. 12   F. 5   J. 11   N. 8
C. 1   G. 2   K. 15   O. 13
D. 9   H. 14   L. 7   P. 4

Acts 1–9 Crossword

Bible Numbers

1. F   6. C
2. A   7. I
3. B   8. H
4. E   9. J
5. G   10. D

Bible Foods Word Search

Birth of Jesus Fill-in

1. Gabriel
2. David
3. virgin
4. angel
5. save, sins

6. Nazareth to Bethlehem
7. amazed
8. Simeon
9. Magi
10. Egypt

More Bible Numbers

1. A
2. D
3. H
4. E
5. G
6. I. She was ninety or ninety-one years old
7. B: Ephesus, Smyrna, Pergamum, Thyatira, Sardis, Philadelphia, Laodicea
8. F: Philip, Bartholomew, Levi, Thomas, Simon Peter, John, Andrew, James, Thaddeus, Thomas, Simon the Zealot, Judas
9. J
10. C

Name That Book

1. c
2. c and d
3. d
4. b
5. d
6. b and d
7. b
8. c
9. c (also Amos mentions Pleiades and Orion)
10. a (twelve times)

Books of the Old Testament Word Search

More Who Said It?

1. G (1 John 1:9)
2. F (John 14:6)
3. E (Isaiah 53:3)
4. H (Genesis 1:27)
5. I (Romans 1:16)
6. C (Job 38:4)
7. A (Psalm 51:1, 4)
8. B (Judges 6:37)
9. J (Ecclesiastes 12:13)
10. D (1 Samuel 1:15)

The Kings of the United Monarchy & Judah Word Search

```
L  S  H  N  S  H  A  I  Z  A  H  A  Q  L  A
Q  J  O  S  I  A  H  O  A  W  Q  J  J  G  S
F  N  I  H  C  A  I  O  H  E  J  E  I  A  W
A  J  B  Z  V  A  H  A  Z  H  H  U  A  S
V  X  O  R  U  I  O  V  Y  O  A  L  R  O  X
B  Q  P  A  F  B  M  V  S  I  W  E  L  G  W
A  Q  S  A  S  C  E  H  Z  V  H  O  X  J  J
H  S  W  B  P  H  A  Z  X  O  M  L  H  T  G
A  L  A  I  B  P  U  M  B  O  N  O  M  A  H
I  K  N  J  H  E  M  O  N  W  A  Y  S  M  N
K  H  A  A  G  M  A  I  J  A  H  E  A  Z  A
E  A  T  H  M  M  K  E  K  A  H  N  C  A  N
Z  I  F  S  Q  A  H  E  I  A  A  V  A  H  Q
E  K  O  V  M  O  H  L  P  S  I  B  H  A  Q
H  E  Z  P  R  H  A  T  S  I  Z  O  E  O  J
F  D  D  A  K  H  G  E  O  J  A  B  H  H  O
M  E  M  X  T  P  H  Z  H  J  M  S  Y  E  N
T  Z  L  A  L  H  X  B  A  E  A  N  Q  J  J
```

Where Is That Story in the Bible?

1. 1 Samuel (See chapter 10)
2. Acts (See chapter 12)
3. Luke (See chapter 2:41–52)
4. Genesis (See chapter 12)
5. Exodus (See chapter 20) and Deuteronomy (See chapter 5)
6. 2 Kings (See chapter 2)
7. Daniel (See chapter 5)
8. John (See chapter 2)
9. Joshua (See chapter 7)
10. Judges (See chapter 4)

People in Jesus's Life

1. B
2. H
3. A
4. I
5. G
6. E
7. D
8. C
9. F
10. J

Quoting Paul

1. faith
2. foolishness
3. gospel
4. crucified
5. Spirit
6. fools
7. bodies
8. patient
9. childhood
10. futile

Book of Revelation Crossword

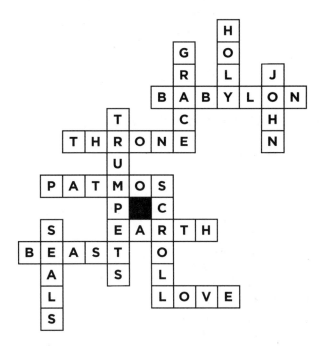

The Kings of the United Monarchy & Israel Word Search

Name That Biblical Location

1. Capernaum
2. Bethany
3. Mount Carmel
4. Garden of Gethsemane
5. Caesarea Philippi
6. Mount Sinai
7. Babylon
8. Nineveh, Tarshish
9. Bethlehem
10. Wilderness or desert

Animals and Other Bible Critters Word Search

```
U S N P G A T I G V C G Z J I
E V N D Z E S H N N A Z D X V
W L G G O C T I A P M F U V W
D I E W F D O H T T E G O R F
P P L V L Z R I E V L K L X Z
L D K B I C K H P R E F D H W
O I Z J J A Y T D D O E S K S
C H O S H S T Q U S L N Z N G
M O O N J W D H N G B E A H G
Y V W X H P J D A S G K O O M
Z S S Y L Y Q E O N E I A H Z
C D H I F C P D Y R Q T I C R
Y R V X X X Y Q H B A W U Q S
E A D V U L T U R E O V C H Y
R P C S W E A S E L E B E G D
P O S P A R R O W V M E P N E
S E E U H S I F O V P J I Y J
O L W M O Z I D N C P R A E B
```

Know Your Bible Sections

1. E
2. I
3. C
4. A
5. F
6. C
7. B
8. G
9. F
10. E
11. A
12. E
13. G
14. I
15. A
16. H
17. D
18. B
19. F
20. B

The Disciples of Jesus

1. Peter and Andrew
2. James and John
3. Sons of Thunder (or Boanerges)
4. Matthew
5. Thomas
6. Judas Iscariot
7. Matthias
8. John
9. James, Judas, Simon
10. John

Holy Week Word Search

The Beatitudes Fill-in

1. spirit
2. comforted
3. meek
4. earth
5. hunger
6. mercy
7. pure
8. God
9. peacemakers
10. persecuted

Heaven Word Search

```
Y K G V M U E Y L S L E G N A
G B Z O J Z A Q A S R E D L E
B Q W H L Z Y J M U R X D F H
S S Z S J D Q E B A X E A J T
A A A X O B T S C K G U V E K
Q G P F T T T U S Q B V M I W
E R A P P E F S D D T P G R R
P E E T H Z S J C L L K R G I
M M Y D E I E A A E A F V X D
W X A O E I R T R S F R G I O
O T R E E P E N K P K E L G
X T U G Y M M J Y R Q E P M P
O P L H N E S E T A G M R E E
Z V B L N I O W D O Z A A G Z
X Z N O O W G G P R B R W S H
W L R L N R M N I F L M P N N
E H Y X W R C F I S T H G I L
T M I L R D D S G S U P S J C
```

Bible Firsts

1. J
2. F
3. G
4. D
5. A
6. B
7. H
8. E
9. C
10. I

Bible "Mounts" of Significance

1. D
2. E
3. F
4. J
5. B
6. A
7. I
8. H
9. C
10. G

Women of the Bible Crossword

How's That Spelled?

1. c
2. b
3. a
4. a
5. a
6. b
7. c
8. b
9. c
10. a

Books of the New Testament Word Search

```
W N O I T A L E V E R D X H U
D S J B I H S W E R B E H D P
L S N A I S S O L O C S V S T
A C T S A O F W Q W E Y U H K
Y N C F P H I L E M O N E P T
P H I L I P P I A N S S G I I
X V X P H I Q J E U S T C P
R U P E P L S V T A R U S B W
Q X R T E J A I L O S N F O G
Y U H E H O M O M S A G Y A J
X U N R O O N A N I D W L U Z
W R P V T I N A H T T A D J A
E G T H A S I T G B T E R O X
H J Y N I S N G Z I Z N B N A
T T S K E I B W A Z M E H I R
T I K H R K N N V U T K P O K
A T P O Q A S V C B V U Q H J
M E C V C T M P J G P L V P K
```

More Animals and Other Bible Critters Word Search

```
M K U Y E F G R L R R M W M G
P A R T R I D G E S A V F R F
Y A G A Z E L L E D M D A B J
T Q D A R B O C A A O S C W C
I K W A H O Y V G S S E G O G
B D W E X K L V T H J I V R I
B F W D Q Z P R O X J J K M W
A Q G B V N I P S D R A Z I L
R C B W G C P V O C Q Q L W V
D N D A H E A T H P Y E G Y H
J O P I R N Z L H X Q G E P A
O E G U T A I N V G G C G P E
T L J Y M E B R J L P U J B D
S E P E S Z K X C O A H Z M P
W M O K I R Z C G L B K Z A N
E A P N A I V L I J L W C L G
W H W O L L A W S R Z U H A B
E C B D O G I H K W C O B O J
```

Putting the Ten Commandments in Order

A. 3	E. 8	I. 10
B. 5	F. 7	J. 9
C. 6	G. 2	
D. 1	H. 4	

Jacob's Family Word Search

How Are They Related? Old Testament

1. grandfather – grandson
2. son – father
3. grandfather – grandson
4. sister-in-law – brother-in-law
5. son-in-law – mother-in-law
6. son – mother
7. grandfather – grandson
8. brothers
9. father – son
10. son – father

How Are They Related? New Testament

1. brothers
2. brothers
3. father – son
4. husband – wife
5. brother – sister
6. mother – son
7. mother – son
8. son – father

Places Jesus Visited Word Search

```
P  Y  W  O  H  C  I  R  E  J  D  M  Z  Z  T
N  S  S  D  L  E  I  F  N  I  A  R  G  G  V
X  B  D  F  F  N  M  E  H  E  L  H  T  E  B
T  E  M  P  L  E  I  J  B  E  P  N  C  T  J
N  X  M  S  L  C  J  N  G  E  R  Y  T  H  X
C  J  D  B  S  L  H  Y  O  O  B  Y  O  S  V
I  A  E  I  E  P  P  O  E  D  I  A  A  E  L
R  J  P  R  M  T  T  W  R  N  I  A  N  M  H
E  G  W  E  U  M  H  A  N  A  V  S  A  A  T
V  A  F  N  R  S  N  S  Q  L  Z  U  I  N  E
I  D  Y  C  E  N  A  R  A  A  X  I  J  E  R
R  A  L  B  C  A  A  L  Y  I  O  F  N  S  A
N  R  H  I  M  M  P  U  E  C  D  A  K  O  Z
A  E  W  N  W  X  P  M  M  R  A  N  A  A
D  N  I  S  E  U  G  O  G  A  N  Y  S  A  N
R  E  K  G  W  I  L  D  E  R  N  E  S  S  C
O  S  Y  E  D  I  S  N  I  A  T  N  U  O  M
J  C  E  E  L  I  L  A  G  G  S  B  X  R  O
```

How Well Do You Know Psalm 23?

The Lord is my **shepherd**, I lack **nothing**.

He makes me lie down in **green pastures**, he leads me beside **still waters**, he refreshes my **soul**.

He guides me along the right **paths** for his name's sake.

Even though I **walk** through the **darkest** valley, I will fear no **evil** for you are with me; your **rod** and your **staff** they comfort me.

You prepare a **table** before me in the presence of my **enemies**. You **anoint** my head with **oil** my **cup** overflows.

Surely **goodness** and **love** will follow me all the **days** of my life, and I will dwell in the **house** of the **Lord** forever.

Theology Terms Word Search

Christmas Word Scramble

1. manger
2. magi
3. cloths
4. baby
5. donkey
6. angels
7. innkeeper
8. camels
9. gifts
10. tidings
11. peace
12. flocks
13. sheep
14. shepherds
15. gold
16. frankincense
17. myrrh
18. star
19. messiah
20. stable

More Theology Terms Word Search

```
E P A T Y C N A R R E N I O E
C F R Z G U Q I M U J F T Q Z
R O R O Z N O I T P M E D E R
E E N E P B N T N E M G D U J
P N C V S I Y V Q E H K R H V
S M O O E U T Y T I R U C E S
S S R I N R R T I R I P S H
E D T Q T C S R A M H C R N V
N S F E L A I E T N I O M W
S K A T W E C L O C I I J N O
U D N C S A S I I N T O Y F R
O Y Q R R K R W F A R I N P S
E T B B Z I Q D L I T B O Y H
T I Y V M Q F U S F T I K N I
H N T S C S B I H H C C O R P
G I I F N I M B C W I K N N M
I R N E R I O N W E N P P A Y
R T U T Y Y S H V B L O O D S
```

Book of Matthew Who Said It?

1. c	4. b	7. c	10. b
2. b	5. c	8. d	
3. c	6. b	9. a	

20/20 Vision

1. H	3. F	5. A	7. B
2. D	4. C	6. E	8. G

Who Wrote What Book?

1. E	4. H	7. A	10. C
2. A	5. A	8. D	
3. G	6. F	9. B	

More How's That Spelled?

1. c	6. c
2. a	7. c
3. c	8. a
4. b	9. b
5. a	10. c

Who Is She?

1. Rachel	4. Delilah	7. Elizabeth	10. Jael
2. Jochebed	5. Hannah	8. Martha	
3. Deborah	6. Phoebe	9. Ruth	

Proverbs Crossword

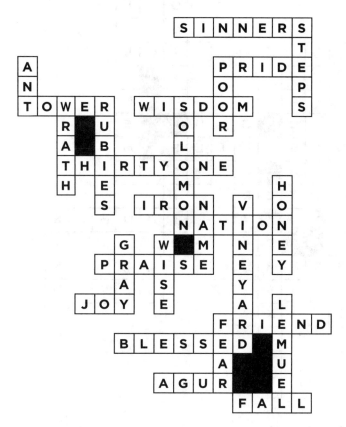

"A" Words

1. Aaron	4. Assyria	7. Alabaster	10. Apocrypha
2. Abba	5. Absalom	8. Alpha	
3. Atonement	6. Agape	9. Amos	

Geography Lesson

1. Northern: Dan; Southern: Beersheba	2. east to west	4. Mount Hermon	7. north
	3. Jordan River	5. Joppa	8. north
		6. Dead Sea	9. Bethany
			10. Rome

Miracles of Jesus Crossword

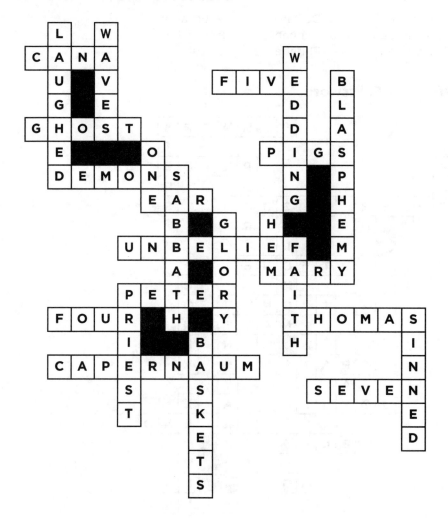

Jerusalem: A City Worth Remembering

1. b
2. a
3. d
4. b
5. c
6. c
7. b
8. a
9. b
10. b

The Book of Daniel Word Search

The Passover of Exodus 12 Word Search

Who Did It?

1. c   2. b   3. a   4. c   5. d   6. d   7. c   8. b   9. d   10. b

Matthew's Genealogy of Jesus Word Search

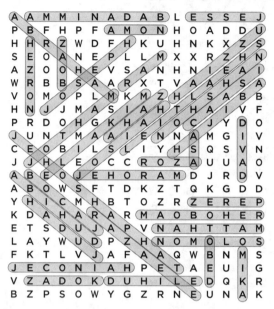

Countries in the Bible (other than Israel) Word Search

Book of Genesis Crossword

How Many?

1. two
2. seven
3. forty
4. eight
5. ten
6. seventy
7. twelve
8. nine
9. thirty
10. two, five

Still More Theology Terms Word Search

Book of Psalms Fill-in

1. Blessed
2. sleep
3. pit
4. majestic
5. angels

6. fool
7. apple
8. rock
9. heavens
10. soul

11. hands, pure
12. light, salvation
13. transgressions
14. Taste
15. righteous

What Love Is

1. patient
2. kind
3. envy
4. boast
5. proud
6. dishonor
7. self-seeking
8. angered
9. wrongs
10. rejoices

Men of the Bible Word Search

More Men of the Bible Word Search

Life of Jesus Crossword

Bible-time Professions Word Scramble

1. baker
2. butler
3. fisherman
4. hunter
5. carpenter
6. shepherd
7. farmer
8. king
9. governor
10. centurion
11. commander
12. soldier
13. scribe
14. goldsmith
15. tentmaker
16. rabbi
17. priest
18. prophet
19. teacher
20. innkeeper

Holy Spirit Fill-in

1. Pentecost
2. body
3. advocate
4. dove
5. grieve
6. fruit
7. weakness
8. deep
9. filled
10. quench

Tabernacle Word Search

```
C T R U O C Y R A U T C N A S
E R Z V I V D N A T S P M A L
D L S N R A T L A T S E I R P
A V H A L V Y T A N R T E Q G
R C O T Z X A M G R N U G L C
G U W L D C Y O K E K A O V H
D R B K N L B N M V W R M E E
W T R W I X O E O B Y J F I R
E A E L A Y N G N U J D E L U
L I A N N O L I N E N L Z N B
L N D I T E M E K D C K U V I
I G O A G W X G E A S N M C M
N P T P Q D B S N T I Y N T L
G T A B L E N R E S S N I K S
E O Y E I E E L A A I C A C A
D D I H C B B G X B W L W K
G S J N A A E C A L P Y L O H
H V I T T G S G N I R E F F O
R T O T Z X A M G R N U G L C
I G O D E N E V A E L N U C M
```

Cities and Towns of the Bible Word Search

```
A H S I H C A L F C G H S E H
B R B D D U W F S H S E D E K
F L E H T E B K A B G E Y E J
N G I B E O N F M N A H T O D
O I T D D K J A A R Z O P S J
L E J A H U M R R M A P U E L
E W C E S B P C I G A S R D M
K L K A Z H P K A M W I N Y T
H T E W P R I E H N C X D B P
S J E H G E E L X H A F N E K
A A E K A U R E O N O A N T G
N S C R O Z K N L H Z K A H A
G H H M U A O R A A R D J L H
A D O Y D S B R R U I G O E E
L O R N G C A E W A M U D H B
K D A A Y U T L S M L M D E R
I F Z H S H C H E E C N I M O
Z Q I T Q J T N J M N N G N N
R R N E R E S H M E H C E H S
I O Q B B E M M A U S D M Z X
```

135

Miracles Crossword

Weights and Measures Word Search

Plants of the Bible Word Search

```
U N A C A C I A B Y E L R A B
L D E E R Q F J E L B M A R B
P I U H U E N I V E P A R G
I P S P I C E S Y N B D S R S
S L A D U L O T U S J T N I M
T Z G A R L I C L Y O P F O Z
A U Y T E T A N A R G E M O P
C A J A D S P W P O P L A R T
H P U E N D Y O Z O Q D L I I
I P S H A H Y O A H N K M T T
O L L W I C K C R A V B R X E
F E I O R C F O G W E E E O L
X N T E O M J T J R B M B Q L
M O N R C A A A P M U L E G I
Q R E O P L G E U S I X F X M
Z F L M O O C C T L S N A E B
P F M A S E U A Y L Y M D L S
Y A P C S C R N O M A N N I C
K S Z Y Y D S U C O R C A P N
Q Z Y S H S Q J C D N O M L A
```

Angel Facts

1. b	6. b
2. c	7. c
3. b	8. c
4. a	9. d
5. b	10. b, d

Words about God Word Scramble

1. glorious
2. creator
3. eternal
4. faithful
5. loving
6. father
7. foreknowledge
8. good
9. gracious
10. holiness
11. light
12. majestic
13. immutable
14. impartial
15. incomprehensible
16. independent
17. infinite
18. invisible
19. jealous
20. judge

"E" Bible Names Word Search

```
I N D D X Z C P U R N A H T E
Q K X X B E Z E K I E L L I V
H F W Q X I T Y P X C R T K E
C V S F L E Z Y H A N A K L E
O K Z U Z A X I M I K A I L E
N A S R H E E H U D H Y Q Z C
E V A P V C L T Q E P N E B B
R G I V Z W Y E T U L Q R L E
K L J B S Y G T A H O I G P F
E R I G K D X K U Z D G A L S
R P E S T H E R D E A P E S B
E L A F S Q O C N H H R U A E
Z A Z M A H L K T R A C E L S
E B I N V T E E O S M L I O H
N E Q F C L B D T X I J G H A
E H U G E A I U Y S A U M R N
B S H M Z T S U H H R S J M N
E I I I U Q A A B O H B A N D
D L L S N S K L Z N P L D Q T
E E E H E E I P X Y E K R B O
Q K X X B E Z E K I E L L I V
E V A P V C L T Q E P N E B B
```

"J" Bible Names Word Search

```
B S E M A J I H A I M E R E J I
T A J E S U S E K M B S L E A J
J O N A T H A N H G J T C Y P G
Y J P B Q U W O B T K O G S M J
M O S B E H Q U B D E T A L A W
L S X S V E E O K K Z H J S O J
R E B U Y J C E B V U E P A H U
H P D J O A M A N Q H H I A N D
S H Z U J Z Y R B O J L V V J A
Z I G H J M V I S X U Q O J S H
J F F N N G R H F J Z N U E W I
B O E B L G A A N N A O J H G Y
J Y N E S P K Z O L I R R O K H
G O D A H W A J L W B G Y R N M
V I E A H U O A M A R O J A F I
H E T L H H A I R J A I R M F K
A A W S N B H X J R J E S S E A
M R O Y B A J E R O B O A M Q I
I J S U I O R Z R H T I D U J
M C R S S E K N E J U D A S W H
E E O W N I H C I O H E J B J E
J J X C Q S U I R A J A G W S J
```

Parables of Jesus Word Scramble

1. **j**ourney
2. deb**tor**s
3. s**o**wer
4. t**a**re**s**
5. mu**st**ard
6. **le**aven
7. **l**amp
8. **d**ragnet
9. trea**su**re
10. wine
11. **ha**r**ve**st
12. **s**amaritan
13. shepherd
14. gate
15. wedding
16. **to**w**e**r
17. **co**i**n**
18. pro**di**ga**l**
19. vine**y**ard
20. virgin**s**

Letters:

j t o r o a s t l e e l d s u h a s t s t o e c n o a y s

A story Jesus told to teach a lesson.

Book of Philippians Crossword

Precious Stones of the Bible Word Search

```
C A R N E L I A N V Z C M Z S
Z K B Y P U X X B D T I D K A
A T D N W I Q Y P L R G Y G E
P C E Q C C P N Y A P U A O D
O T L P P A C O P T A T B I E
T R L E S E R S Z E E P A Y R
U J I A S N T B D M D M K V I
D E U R C V Q I U E O W R P H
C D M L B Y C H L N R N E D P
Y S Q S G H N K D O C U G L P
Y J A S P E R O W Q S L G L A
A M E T H Y S T D B Q Y E I S
O F T N A M A D A E E J R G L
G S U R F E S D H G C R M H P
Z I E M G U I Y Y T C L Y M C
E Q A V I R H G R L N V A L V
C S N D E V S L A B E I F H D
G Z R B L A R O C L T B C U C
T A M L S A R D O N Y X E A V
S A B V V N C R Y S T A L F J
```

Trees of the Bible Word Search

```
S V A L O E S J O L R O M C P
Q Y P L T N E X L B O X Y I Z
W G C J H L R R I F F P N M W
A I I A P A U O V Q R E A K B
U L L P M C Z G E E V Z A D G
Z D A L I O U E S P W G S O C
T Y U Q O N R S L S B R P E F
N L E X E W Q E D X I H D I M
D Z J C P X S R V K E A G Q D
W Z J I U G J Z J R R B M J K
X M U N H O K A A S H A R B Z
Y E N N H M A N D N O M L A I
O G I A T T H K O V R G F Y I
Y S P M N M N D A T E R N R V
O G E O R R Y I M Q U O D R A
C Q R N X M Q R B I B O K E I
W U T L Z P L M T E D B C B C
M I G P O P L A R L R C S L A
C H E S T N U T P M E E N U C
P O M E G R A N A T E X T M A
Q Y P E X L B O X Y I Z N M W
N L E Q E D X I H D I M A K B
```

140

In the Bible or Not?

1. Yes. Proverbs 14:23
2. No. Probably from a sermon by John Wesley, 1778
3. No. From a song by William Cowper, 1773
4. Yes. Proverbs 21:19
5. Yes. Job 39:13
6. No.
7. No. Probably from an Aesop's fable
8. Yes. Psalm 133:1
9. No. Mahatma Gandi said this in 1929: "Hate the sin and not the sinner."
10. Yes. Job 19:20

Words Associated with Jesus Word Search

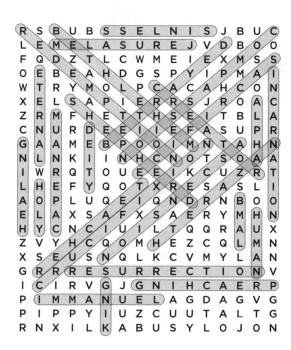

Where's That Quote?

1. c	7. b
2. b	8. a
3. a	9. d
4. d	10. a
5. d	
6. c	

Bible Firsts Crossword

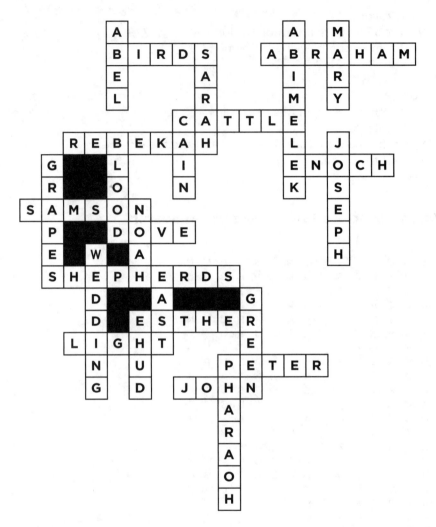

Jesus Quote Fill-in

1. bread
2. fish, people
3. meek
4. salt
5. enemies
6. heaven
7. plentiful
8. Sabbath, Sabbath
9. will
10. little children

"M" Biblical Names and Places

```
M A R T H A H A L E S U H T E M
I B T T T H M A T T H E W N R B
D E R R D L A M E I L A H C I M
I M L A C Q E R H A B I R E M
A N O T K G T C A Z O L O T I N
B H V D I L A I D L E A H C I M
D P D J A A D D M A G D A L A V
X O B M F G H B F C A I B Q J M
O P J M A N A S S E H M W T E G
M E L C H I Z E D E K V W S X M
H M M A M R E S I S C Z H Q I R
Z E Q Z N R J R X K I A Y C F S
G L H D Q Z L V A M C H H R S K
X C A S J P B I I H N A P A A P
K H L Y Q V N R X S H H I M X M
W I E V F O I Q U S U H Q R E M
Y A P F D A Y H E G T T Z H O M
K H H E M T C Y O T A N E A B Y
R X C P Q L B G A U K N B L O O
A A A B A J A M L V H W B T I C
M I M M G M V N H T K S O B G M
```

Biblical Prophets Word Search

```
E Z E K I E L O A H S I L E S
W M J V M E D N B H O S E A I
E L I J A H N A S E C L K H N
K V J A P T X I D W D J E A M
R N H B X R U D L Y T U H O V
E K A X Z Z N Q I J K U L Z J
O Q I L Q M V N K U M N Z N O
A G A H H A C I M L E I N A D
H I S Y Q K L X Z Z B C K L A
B H I C P Z E C H A R I A H J
I C E E E D Q M I A Y S W E R
Y A X U C O H V E Y H O R W J
G L Q X K A G K H A C E F O K
P A D K D U A V I A M W N V F
P M W L X V K N K I I A P I M
C L U Q U D A K A V H D A N M
Z H Q Y D H O H A I B G A P R
Q X N U P Z U B R B G Q R B W
C E G E S O M A T A A A F N O
M G Z U M G G C H M Q H G Y R
```